CHURCH ORGANS

CHURCH ORGANS

A Guide to Selection and Purchase

John K. Ogasapian

BAKER BOOK HOUSE
Grand Rapids, Michigan 49506

COVER PHOTOGRAPHS: Upper left: First United Methodist Church, Corvallis, Oregon; tracker-action instrument built by the Noack Organ Company, Georgetown, Massachusetts, 1980; **Center:** Two-manual reed organ manufactured by the Farrand Organ Company, Detroit, Michigan, 1903; **Lower left:** Rodgers Classic Organ, Series 205, combining pipework and electronically generated voices, Rodgers Organ Company, Hillsboro, Oregon; **Lower right:** Fitzkee Memorial Organ, Chapel of the Good Samaritan, Lutheran Social Services—East Region, Lititz, Pennsylvania; built by E. and G. G. Hook in 1867; acquired through the Organ Clearing House; restoration by James R. McFarland and Company, Millersville, Pennsylvania.

To my Mother and Father
Marion and Karekin Ogasapian
And in Memory of my Mother- and Father-in-Law
Marguerite and Roscoe Hill

Contents

List of Illustrations   9

Acknowledgments   11

Preface   13

1. Costs   17
2. Architectural Considerations   21
3. The Organ in Today's Worship   25
4. Pipe Organs   29
5. Electronic Organs   39
6. Reed Organs   45
7. Rebuilding an Old Organ   49
8. Maintenance Considerations   55
9. The Role of the Consultant   61
10. Summary of Pertinent Factors   65
11. Weighing the Options   73
12. The Process of Recycling   79
13. How Much Organ Do You Need?   87
14. Selecting the Builder   93
15. Contracting with the Builder   99
16. Some Elements of Tonal Design   103
17. Building the Organ—A Sketch   111
18. Further Reading   117

Appendix 1—A Selection of Stoplists   121

Appendix 2—A Glossary of Terms   129

Illustrations

Page

1. Calvin Christian Reformed Church, Oak Lawn, Illinois (Schlicker). Photo by John Mulder.

2. First United Methodist Church (Henderson Chapel), Lufkin, Texas (Austin). Photo by Photo-World.

6. Christ Episcopal Church, Overland Park, Kansas (McManis). Photo by Warner Studio.

8. Christ Lutheran Church, Charlotte, North Carolina (Bozeman-Gibson). Photo by Tommy Clay.

12. St. Mary's Episcopal Church, East Providence, Rhode Island (Roche).

15. Lutheran Center, Pittsburgh, Pennsylvania (Möller). Photo by Armand F. Latour.

18. Trinity Presbyterian Church, Indianola, Iowa (Dobson). Photo by Eaton's Studio.

22. St. Paul's Episcopal Church, Brookline, Massachusetts (Bozeman-Gibson). Photo by Hutchins Photography.

24. Rockledge Presbyterian Church, Rockledge, Florida (Reuter).

27. Danforth Chapel, University of Kansas, Lawrence (Reuter).

28. St. Patrick's Episcopal Church, Washington, D.C. (Holtkamp).

32. Photos and schematics of organ pipes (Dan Malda).

35. Calvin Christian Reformed Church, Oak Lawn, Illinois (Schlicker). Photo by John Mulder.

37. Ascension Lutheran Seminary, Philadelphia, Pennsylvania (Zimmer).

40. Organ console (Saville).

41. Organ console (Baldwin).

Page

43. Organ console (Allen).

46. Free reeds. Photo by Dan Malda.

47. Hillside Congregational Church, Cornish, Maine (Mason and Hamlin). Photo by Mr. and Mrs. Q. Regestein.

47. Shapleigh Baptist Church, Shapleigh, Maine (Mason and Hamlin). Photo by Mr. & Mrs. Q. Regestein.

51. St. Mary's Church, Charleston, South Carolina (Jardine). Photo by William Van Pelt.

51. Sacred Heart Church, Marlborough, New Hampshire (Hook and Hastings). Photo by William Van Pelt.

52. Grace Episcopal Church, Amherst, Massachusetts (Stuart). Photo by Delia H. Baroni.

56. Dilworth Lutheran Church, Dilworth, Minnesota (Johnson).

58. Leather pneumatics.

66. St. Anthony's Roman Catholic Church, Upland, California (Rosales).

69. St. James Lutheran Church, Kansas City, Missouri (Reuter).

70. Rodgers Classic Series 205.

76. St. Andrew's Church, Marblehead, Massachusetts (unknown builder).

80. Pearson Memorial United Methodist Church, White Horse, New Jersey (Steere).

81. Trinity Episcopal Church, Redlands, California (Jardine).

84. St. John's Church, North Charleston, South Carolina (Hook and Hastings).

84. Prince of Peace Lutheran Church, West Claremont, New Hampshire (Midmer).

84. St. Paul's Episcopal Church, Woodville, Mississippi (Erben).

84. Trinity Lutheran Church, Columbia, South Carolina (unknown builder).

86. The Church of Our Savior, Montpelier, Virginia (Mann and Trupiano).

90. Edgerton House, Hanover, New Hampshire (Noack).

106. Christ the King Lutheran Church, Nashua, New Hampshire (Wissinger).

113. First Hungarian Reformed Church, Munhall, Pennsylvania (Schantz).

Acknowledgments

Many people helped, in one way or another, to make this book possible, especially: Wilson Barry, Edgar A. Boadway, John A. Goodwin, Alan M. Laufman, Earl Miller, Robert Newton, Fritz Noack, Barbara J. Owen, Robert J. Reich, Lawrence Trupiano, William T. Van Pelt III, and the many builders who graciously responded to my request for photographs and stoplists of their work.

Gordon De Young, my editor at Baker Book House, and my friend, has been a veritable partner in this work, and a constant source of patience and good counsel. The glossary at the end of the book is largely his contribution. He is also responsible for the attractive layout and the informative captions which appear with the photographs.

Again, for the third time, I record my love for, and gratitude to, my wife Nancy and my daughter Lisa. As usual, both have been supportive, helpful, patient, and understanding; no man has ever been more blessed in his family than have I.

This is a book for clergymen and laypersons who are faced with a decision about an organ for their church. To the extent that it assists them in making that decision in the best possible manner, it will have fulfilled its purpose and justified the contributions of all those listed, as well as the hopes of the author.

John Ogasapian
Pepperell, Massachusetts
November 30, 1982

11

Preface

Buying a church organ is a once-in-a-lifetime event for most music committee members. Although they hear the instrument Sunday after Sunday, meditate to its quiet background, listen to it play the prelude, postlude, and offertory, and sing to its accompaniment, either from the congregation or the choirloft, few laypersons understand the differences between the various types of instruments, or the principles on which organs operate. Few are familiar with organ terminology, or have any real idea of those factors that determine whether or not a given organ, or type of organ, will prove to be satisfactory to the needs of their church. Yet those same persons may well be called on to serve as music or property committee members and be faced with the decision of whether to repair or replace an old organ; of deciding which of the several types of instruments will be best for their church; in short, of passing on what may well be the single largest item of a church's furnishings.

No wonder most laypersons feel uncomfortable in such a situation. It has fallen to them to decide the best way of spending a considerable sum of the congregation's money: funds that as yet may not even have been raised. The instrument must meet the church's worship needs. It must be within the parish's fiscal reach. It must be of sufficient quality to attract a competent organist. And, the committee may well hope, it will be capable of "anchoring" a vital and growing music program.

That is quite an order. Buying a church organ is a serious matter for the large and affluent congregation, presumably able to absorb the cost of a poor decision. Normally a parish with resources at that level will engage a consultant to work with the church in determining the proper design, choosing the proper builder, and generally, as the church's representative, overseeing the project from its inception to the instrument's dedication.

Smaller churches will usually find themselves in less fortunate circumstances. Their budget will be lower and may not permit the luxury of retaining a consultant to shepherd the project along. Their committees will often be unaware that basic and preliminary advice is cheaply and readily available. Members of the committee will not be sure if they need a consultant (and at certain stages of *any* organ project, competent, disinterested advice can be of great assistance). They may have the good fortune to encounter informed advice from a local professional organist; or they may have the misfortune to encounter *un*informed advice from a local professional organist. Playing the organ well is no more guarantee of knowledge of its design and construction than driving an automobile well assures one of the capability to design and engineer a vehicle.

Most often the committee will be forced to rely on the recommendations of a specific firm or its representative, who quite obviously will have a vested interest in making a sale. Most such representatives are honest and scrupulous; as in every field, a few are not. But many, if not most, are far less well informed about organs in general, and the needs of churches in particular, than they are about their company's product.

This book aims to provide committees with a convenient source of competent and disinterested advice to assist them in making a decision, not in favor of one organ as against another, but rather in favor of the organ that will best serve the needs of their church, both present and future.

The first chapters are devoted to such general considerations as costs, acoustics, and the use of the organ in the church. There follow chapters devoted to the types of instruments, describing how they work, their terminology, and the advantages and drawbacks of each type. The next chapter deals with "recycling" old organs for both artistic and economic reasons. Then follow considerations of main-

This small two-manual, tracker-action organ built by the M. P. Moller Company, Hagerstown, Maryland, was recently installed in the Lutheran Center, Pittsburgh.

tenance and servicing, and the use of consultants. After a summary of the material presented to that point, five chapters present workable procedures for the committee to follow at each stage of an organ project.

This book will assist the reader in comparing initial and long-term costs, reviewing musical considerations, and in general delineating the best course for the organ-purchase committee to follow. This book will not make the reader an organ expert, or even an extraordinarily well-informed organ amateur. It cannot impart the depth of knowledge that requires years of experience and study. But what it can and will do is give the reader the information he or she needs to weigh all the relevant factors, determine if and when he or she needs on-the-spot advice to make a proper decision about this or that, discuss intelligently the instrument and its use in church, and finally, arrive at the best possible decision for his or her church and its special needs.

1

Costs

The first thing to be kept in mind is that any kind of organ—putting aside for a moment that aesthetic intangible that makes it a work of art, a failure, or something in between—is a relatively simple machine, given the technology of our time. It is nowhere near so complex, for instance, as the cars we drive, still less the computers that figure our monthly bank balances.

If that is so, some may ask why an organ is so much more expensive than a car, or a computer. After all, one can get several top quality minicomputers with every conceivable accessory, or a fully equipped midsize car, for the price of but one or two stops, or ranks of pipes, brand new, from a top-rank organ builder. To put it another way, the price of a new, very modest two-manual pipe organ from that same top builder, will buy a comfortable suburban home situated on a good bit of acreage. A stock-model electronic organ, minimally acceptable for church use, will be found comparable in price to a luxury car, again fully equipped.

On reflection, the answer is obvious. Cars, computers, and even houses can be built in quantity on mechanized assembly lines. Pipe organs, by contrast, are custom items, and must be built largely by hand by master craftsmen, working alone, or in small shops. Each pipe organ is made to order for the room that is to house it. That does not mean that an organ built for one church cannot be moved

The building of a fine pipe organ requires skilled workmanship in a variety of fields, including that of cabinetry. In recent years many organists and organ builders have once again recognized the importance, both functionally and visually, of an organ case. Shown here is the encased pipe organ of the Trinity Presbyterian Church, Indianola, Iowa, built by Lynn A. Dobson, Lake City, Iowa.

to another. In fact, as we shall see, that very thing is done regularly and successfully.

The factor of reliability is also reflected in the high price of an organ, especially a pipe organ, although even the electronic organs suitable for church use (as distinct from home-model organs, with their array of rhythm sections, Hawaiian guitar slides, etc.) are priced relatively high. In the manufacture of church organs there is no margin for mediocre or indifferent workmanship, the degree of quality variance that is sometimes allowed in mass-produced items, even computers. Church organs cannot be compared to home stereo systems. Churches expect their organs to function reliably every Sunday. A member of your church may well think nothing of his new-model car being in a repair or maintenance facility on the average of one day every six weeks; he may and often does tolerate his business computer being "down" an average of one day a month. But on Sunday morning he will probably be "put out" if the organ, which may well have lain unused throughout the week in an empty, badly insulated church building, does not spring to life at the touch of a switch and function flawlessly throughout the service. Even a malfunction occuring as infrequently as one Sunday during the year is irritating. Unflawed reliability is not an unreasonable demand; however, meeting such a requirement requires a care in choice of materials and manufacture that is rarely lavished on an item in our day of mass-production.

Thus, in the case of the pipe organ especially, what the buyer pays for is the craftsmanship that brings reliability.

The buyer also pays for artistry. A fine pipe organ is as much a work of art as is a stained glass window. In fact, it is such not only to the ear, but also to the eye; for if it is properly encased and fronted, a pipe organ is equally a visual work of art. And, as will be pointed out in subsequent chapters, more to the concern of any committee working within budgetary limitations, a pipe organ, properly designed, installed, and maintained, will literally last *for centuries*. Of all this, more later.

Specific dollar figures have not been mentioned, not so much out of solicitude for the reader's blood pressure, but rather because no quoted figure can be stable in the normally unstable economy in which we all live. The prices of all types of organs are relatively high. With organs, as with anything else, nobody gets any more than he or she is willing to pay for. A poor organ by a local builder whose price is as low as his reputation will not justify the money spent in the end. No organ is priced so cheaply that its dreadful sound and lack of reliability can be tolerated.

One final point. From time to time one hears how a fine piano is preferable for worship to a poor organ, "poor" being variously defined as an electronic rather than a pipe organ, or one with just a few stops. I readily admit to a love for fine pianos and a concomitant aversion to poor organs; however, I have yet to see a worship tradition in which a piano could answer the needs for the variety of accompaniments and moods needed in praise, prayer, and personal examination, at least over a period of time. The culture of modern Christianity and Reformed Judaism, to say nothing of their history, demands otherwise. Thus, notwithstanding opinions to the contrary from some very fine and respected church musicians, I must counsel strongly against settling for a piano, even on a temporary basis, without giving very careful thought to all the ramifications of such a course.

2

Architectural Considerations

Some of the material in this chapter will be of most interest to committee members whose church is planning, building, or completing a new edifice. Other material will assist those who worship in an older building. Most of it, however, is quite applicable to both situations. The subject deserves careful consideration.

Recent styles in some of the more progressive schools of church music composition make use of electronic backgrounds and taped accompaniments. For that purpose, a good sound system will, of course, be necessary. For normal "public address," the usual needs of worship—preaching, choral music, the support of congregational singing—any well-designed sanctuary seating fewer than 1,000 should not need a sound system as an acoustical support.

It seems almost unnecessary to observe that churches were singing, preaching, and worshiping long before the invention of the vacuum tube, let alone the transistor. A church that requires a sound system to carry the music from the choir loft, or the spoken word from the pulpit, is a poorly designed church or one whose natural acoustics have been artificially dampened. In such a church no amount of electronic gadgetry will restore the natural "halo" that carries music and message.

Most churches that have spent thousands of dollars on sound systems have had to do so because some committee in the not-too-distant past "beautified" the church with carpeting, draperies and

The installation of a new organ often provides the opportunity for consideration of architectural and acoustical elements as they affect worship. This two-manual, thirty-one stop, tracker-action pipe organ was installed in St. Paul's Episcopal Church, Brookline, Massachusetts, in 1982. It was built by Bozeman-Gibson & Co., Deerfield, New Hampshire. The hardwood floors and the smooth plaster insure a reverberant sanctuary in which the organ can be heard at its best.

possibly "acoustical" tile, in the mistaken notion that "perfect" acoustics, whatever they may be, are synonymous with no reverberation or natural resonance. Difficult though it may be from a political point of view, serious consideration should be given to stripping carpet from hardwood floors, discarding draperies (which in nine cases out of ten are inconsistent with the church's architecture, anyway), and removing acoustical wall and ceiling tiles.

Contrary to popular belief, newer floor tiling is as sturdy and easy to maintain as any carpeting. An aisle runner of thin pile will cut down on the noise of footsteps. Louvers can be installed to prevent the sun from streaming though windows. If removing wall and ceiling tiles is out of the question, at least give them a coat of hard surfacing material.

Sometimes the installation of a new organ and remodeling and redecorating of the sanctuary go hand in hand. Older churches should resist the temptation to "spruce up" their sanctuaries with anything other than paint for walls and ceiling, and sealer for floors. Beware of the interior decorator who insists on wall-to-wall carpeting.

Pew cushions are actually of little real concern, since fully clothed people sitting on them will absorb as much sound as cushions on empty pews do.

The fear of echo and its attendant distortion is usually overemphasized. Seldom, if ever, does such a problem occur, other than in circular buildings and in long, narrow, high gothic and gothic-revival buildings; and even then, only in large examples.

Other than the one cited earlier relative to electronic background, the only concern that should prompt consideration of a sound system in a modest or even comparatively generous-sized sanctuary is for parishioners who have hearing impairment. Systems exist in which certain, or even all, pews are wired for sound (which may be turned on or off), with small speakers in the hymnal racks. Another system, which has proven to be less successful overall, because of human reluctance, involves giving hearing-impaired parishioners small battery-operated receivers with earphones attached, enabling them to sit wherever they wish and still "tune-in" to the word and music being literally transmitted from the front of the sanctuary.

Concerning the matter of those with impaired hearing, it is necessary to bear in mind (and those who make and sell hearing aids are well aware of this) that there are numerous kinds of deafness, and no *one* system can address the entire range of them. Most problems result not from a diminished sense of hearing, per se, but rather from the attenuation of certain frequencies, usually the high ones, causing the sound of speech to become garbled and unintelligible. That is why a "deaf" person may well be able to hear a telephone ringing, but be unable to make out what is being said by the party at the other end of the line once he or she picks the receiver up.

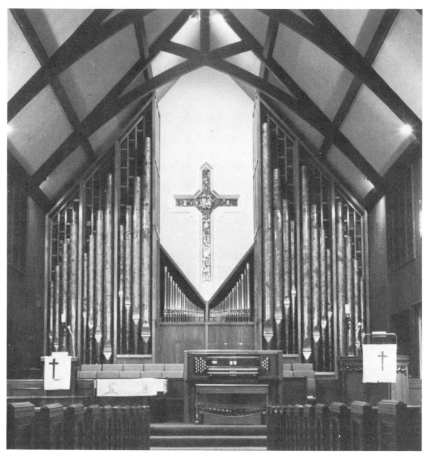

If the console of an electro-pneumatic organ is installed with sufficient cable, it can be moved to different locations. The console of this organ in the Rockledge Presbyterian Church, Rockledge, Florida is shown in position for a recital. The instrument was built and installed by the Reuter Organ Company, Lawrence, Kansas. Note the large flamed copper 16′ pipes in the facade. The smaller pipes of the mixture in the center are made of burnished tin.

In short, simply amplifying sound from pulpit and choirloft will be of little or no assistance to those with hearing impairment. A system that will address their needs will be expensive, carefully designed, and involve individual speaker units or receivers.

Thus, for all practical purposes, no sound system is probably needed in the great majority of churches. It is far better, and cheaper, to keep the sanctuary's natural liveliness and resonance intact by avoiding carpeting, absorbent wall and ceiling materials, and draperies.

3

The Organ in Today's Worship

An organ purchase committee must concern itself with several elements of modern worship as it sets about considering its options in obtaining an organ. Four specific needs stand out.

Support of Congregational Singing

The organ will be most used, and *most importantly* used, in supporting congregational singing. Today's congregations expect and need strong support from the organ. Brightness, clarity, and liveliness of ensemble are far more necessary than sheer volume of sound. No matter how loud it may be, a dull and ponderous tone will stifle the enthusiasm of the congregation in its effort to praise God in song.

It is appropriate here to mention something that will be emphasized later. As a committee progresses in its task of selecting an organ, it reaches the stage where it makes visits to hear examples of organs. Surprisingly, only a limited amount of information can be gathered by traveling around to listen to the work of various builders in empty churches. There is simply no way to tell how well a given organ will support congregational singing on Sunday morning by listening to it from the back pew of a vacant sanctuary on a Tuesday evening! Hear the instrument at work on a Sunday morning, with people in the pews and a choir in the loft.

Accompaniment of Choirs and Soloists

An organ capable of accompanying a choir or soloist is not necessarily one with a great variety of stops of different qualities. But it must have some sort of secondary, softer ensemble, in addition to the brighter, more present sound needed for accompanying congregational singing.

Solo Music

Preludes, offertories, and postludes should be integral parts of the worship service. Generally an organ which adequately supports congregational singing and accompanies choirs and soloists will also be suitable for the solo music used in other parts of the service.

Recitals

Last, and least, as we shall see, the organ should be adequate to play enough literature so that it can give a respectable account of itself in a recital.

Some readers may ask why recitals should be the *least* of considerations. Others will ask why they should receive *any* consideration. The answer to both questions, surprisingly enough, is the same. Any organ suitable for service accompaniments (congregation, choir, and soloists) will also be adequate for service music (preludes, offertories, and postludes). If it meets these requirements it will also serve well as an instrument for recitals. I speak from experience as both a church musician and an organ recitalist.

Even the smallest well-designed organ is capable of playing literature as well as service music. Moreover, as we shall see later, a large church building need not have a large organ to be adequately equipped. In short, there are no such instruments as well-designed *church* organs, and well-designed *concert* organs. There are only well-designed organs . . . and some that are not so well designed.

A well-designed one-manual pipe organ can support congregational singing, accompany choirs and soloists, and be used for service music. It can also serve as an instrument for recitals. This small pipe organ was built by the Reuter Organ Company, Lawrence, Kansas, and installed in the Danforth Chapel of the University of Kansas in Lawrence.

This pipe organ in St. Patrick's Episcopal Church, Washington, D.C., has three divisions: Great Organ, Swell Organ, and Pedal Organ. The divisions are readily discernible by the disposition of the pipes and by the swell shades. This instrument, with mechanical key action and electric stop action, was designed and built by the Holtkamp Organ Company, Cleveland, Ohio.

4

Pipe Organs

In essence, a pipe organ is an instrument with one or more keyboards (or *manuals*) and a pedalboard, each controlling a *division,* or group of *stops.* A stop is made up of a set, or *rank,* of pipes through which wind is blown to create musical tone. Every stop has one pipe for each note on the keyboard (except for stops known as *mixtures,* which will be discussed shortly). In other words, if there are five stops, there will be five different pipes capable of sounding each note, alone or together. The pipes differ as to character, volume, or even actual pitch, depending on the shape of the pipe, its length, cross-sectional area, mouth size and shape, wind pressure, and even more somewhat arcane variables which we need not go into here, thus allowing for variety in quality and volume, depending on which stop or combination of stops the organist turns on, or *draws.*

The normal compass of a manual keyboard (its range of notes from lowest to highest) is either 56, 58, or 61 notes, beginning at the "C" two octaves below "Middle C," and carrying up to the "G" two and a half or the "C" three octaves above, or the "A" in between those two notes, depending on the design of the builder or consultant. In point of fact, there is very little literature calling for the top half-octave—too little, in the opinion of many, to justify the expense of the notes.

The normal range of the pedalboard is from "C"—an octave lower than the lowest manual "C" (but written the same as that note)—to either "F" or "G", thirty or thirty-two notes higher. Here again, so little literature calls for the high "F#" and "G" that having the extended compass seems to many to be uneconomical.

Thus, an organ with ten stops in the manuals and one in the pedal division will have from 590 to 642 pipes (again, assuming that there are no mixtures).

The character of each stop is described by its nomenclature. A Viola, for instance, will be stringlike (no stop really imitates, or is intended by its maker to imitate, the actual instrument); a Flute, obviously, will be flutelike. An Oboe, Clarinet, or Trumpet suggests the tone of the respective instrument. Remember, the intent is not to *imitate* the orchestral sounds; rather, to suggest a similarity; sometimes a rather tenuous one, to tell the truth.

Diapasons, or Principals, produce the traditional organ sound: the tone quality that we associate with the instrument, suggestive of no orchestral counterpart.

Along with the name, a number is engraved on the stop knob or tablet. This number indicates the pitch of the stop, and corresponds to the approximate length (in the case of normal, open flue pipes) of the lowest and longest pipe in the rank. Readers who may have had a high-school physics course will recall that the longer a tube (or pipe) is, the lower will be its resonating frequency (or pitch). The number is approximately accurate for a set of open pipes, such as an Open Diapason. An 8' rank of the latter will have a lowest pipe with a speaking length of about eight feet. Stopped ranks (pipes which have their ends closed off either by a cap or by a stopper so that they yield a different tone quality) will be physically half as long. That is, the lowest pipe of an 8' Stopped Diapason will actually be only four feet in speaking length. Nevertheless, the number engraved on the knob or tablet is *always* the pitch-level, regardless of the actual physical length of the lowest pipe.

A stop of 16' pitch will sound an octave lower than one of 8'; a 4' stop an octave higher, and a 2' stop still another octave higher.

Some stops are made in odd fractional lengths: pitch levels of 2⅔', 1⅗', and 1⅓'. Such stops are called *mutations*. They are intended for combining with 8' stops and bring out or add overtones to the latter, producing a variety of colors for solo work.

Still other stops are engraved not with a number but rather with a roman numeral. The numeral indicates that the stop is a *mixture,* sounding for each of its notes a carefully determined combination of pipes simultaneously. The number of pipes for each note is indicated by the numeral. Mixtures serve to clarify and even out the ensemble of a division. Their composition normally does not remain the same from lowest note to highest, but rather changes, or "breaks," periodically, so that the lower range is brightened, the middle strengthened, and the high range is restrained and kept from becoming shrill.

Occasionally, although not as frequently as in years past, organs are built so that by means of an electrical switch, a single rank of pipes is made to serve at more than one pitch. Such stops are called *unit stops,* and whole organs (*unit organs*) have been so built. There are distinct compromises and dangers in this practice, and most builders of repute frown on it for all but the softest stops, or in the smallest of instruments. Even there, fewer stops, carefully voiced, are far better than many unit stops. If the principle is applied, it should be restricted to a soft stop or two, and then only at unison and octave pitches. In past years, builders have tried to derive mutations from unit ranks. It cannot be done. Mutations are tuned differently than unisons, and the same pipe simply cannot be made to serve both purposes with even minimal acceptability.

Unit organs *have* been made that are quite effective. Theatre organs of bygone days were largely unit organs. Far better for church use, however, would be a few stops, each a single full rank of pipes, properly scaled and voiced to do its job, than a dozen or more stops derived from a small number of ranks, each of which has been compromised in an attempt to make it do double or triple duty.

The pipes of each division stand on a *windchest.* The windchest, often referred to simply as the "chest," contains the apparatus by which valves under the pipes are opened, either mechanically or electrically, letting wind into them and causing them to speak. The wind is delivered to the windchest from the *reservoir,* a bellows-like box, which serves to steady the wind and give it a predetermined and constant pressure. The reservoir, in turn, receives the wind from the *blower,* a large fan driven by an electric motor.

The wind pressure of an organ is quite light, usually from 2½ to 3 inches (a pressure sufficient to raise a column of water from 2½ to 3 inches in a tube).

A valve or *pallet* may be opened either electrically or mechani-

A metal pipe, with its felted cap.

A tapered pipe of spotted metal.

PARTS OF METAL FLUE PIPE

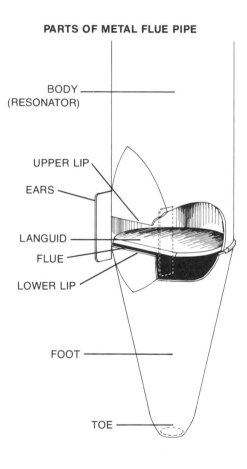

BODY
(RESONATOR)

UPPER LIP

EARS

LANGUID

FLUE

LOWER LIP

FOOT

TOE

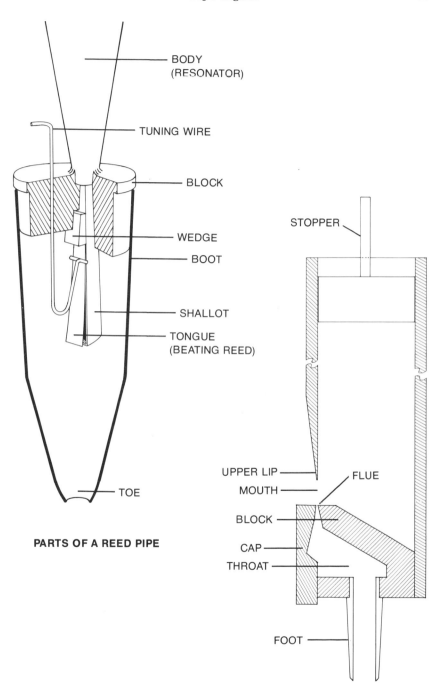

BODY
(RESONATOR)

TUNING WIRE

BLOCK

WEDGE

BOOT

SHALLOT

TONGUE
(BEATING REED)

TOE

PARTS OF A REED PIPE

STOPPER

UPPER LIP

FLUE

MOUTH

BLOCK

CAP

THROAT

FOOT

PARTS OF A WOOD FLUE PIPE

cally. Before explaining the differences in actions, let us review for a moment the principle involved in the overall operation of the organ. When a stop is drawn (on), all its pipes are placed in readiness for playing. In an instrument with electric or electropneumatic action (the latter having small exhaust bellows which cushion the suddenness of direct electrical action), drawing a stop energizes a magnet which either directly, or by means of the exhaust bellows, places the rank of pipes into readiness.

In mechanical- or *tracker*-action instruments, the pulling of the stop knob moves a lever connected to a thin strip of wood called a *slider,* causing it to move lengthwise. The slider contains holes drilled in the same pattern as those in the *toeboard,* on which the pipes stand. The movement of the slider allows its holes to be aligned with those in the toeboard, opening a clear channel for the wind, once the pallets are opened. Pushing a key causes the pallet to open, admitting air to the channel into the pipe foot through the aligned holes in the slider and the toeboard, and forces the pipe to speak.

In a direct electric action, the key, like the stop control, simply closes a circuit, energizing a magnet. In electropneumatic action, the magnet again causes an exhaust pouch to snap shut, and the motion of the closing opens the windway. In mechanical, or tracker, action, the motion of depressing the key is relayed through thin strips of wood, called *trackers* (hence the term *tracker action*) and *squares* (90-degree pivots), *rollers,* and other mechanical linkages, directly to the pallets.

The principles involved here are not difficult to grasp, and all three systems are quite reliable, albeit of quite different life expectancies. However, there are both qualitative and quantitative considerations that churches intending to contract for a pipe organ must study in order to determine which type of action will best suit their needs. Even though the sounding portions of the organ, wind under pressure and pipes, are substantially the same in all pipe organs, and would appear to be the two important components of the three major ones, other factors must also be considered.

The type of key action and stop action chosen will affect the sound in many ways, some subtle and some not so subtle. Moreover, the action portions of an organ take the most abuse over its active lifetime. Therefore, when rebuilding or replacement of the organ becomes necessary (decades down the line), it will most probably result from deterioration or failure of the action.

The actual pipes, by the way, represent a far smaller portion of

Use of electrically operated slider chests (which do not utilize leather pneumatics) allows placement of the console some distance from the chests and their pipes. This encased organ of the Calvin Christian Reformed Church, Oak Lawn, Illinois, utilizes such slider chests. It was manufactured and installed by the Schlicker Organ Company, Buffalo, New York, 1982.

the organ's cost than the myriad components of the action. Thus, it is appropriate to stop and consider briefly the pros and cons of various types of actions for a pipe organ. The mechanical principles of each type have been explained sufficiently for our purposes. Electric actions (and I shall use the term, for the sake of convenience, to include both direct electric and electropneumatic types) allow the console or keydesk (where the organist sits) to be located at some distance from the organ's chests and pipework. Electric actions also allow the organ to be divided and fit into various separated and sometimes oddly shaped spaces. Therefore electric actions may appear to be an excellent choice for the sake of convenience and versatility. In point of fact, however, the generally regarded advantage is a pronounced *dis*advantage.

From a functional and musical point of view, it is far better that organist, pipework, and choir be in close proximity. Only in such a situation can the organist properly gauge the balance of choir and organ. To squeeze pipes into broom closet-type chambers, yards away from the player, is to reduce the effectiveness both of the organ and the organist. Thus the very limitation imposed by tracker action, which requires that keydesk and pipework be in close proximity and prohibits the separation of the pipes, makes for a better musical result.

Moreover, electric actions have a limited life expectancy. About forty years is the most one can count on before leathers and wiring begin to fail and massive work is required. By contrast, tracker actions function for a century or more with only normal maintenance and occasional and relatively uncomplicated repair. The simple direct action of levers and mechanical motion is an easy principle for any layman to grasp. Numerous old trackers in small-town churches have served faithfully with occasional repairs by a local resident whose knowledge of organ maintenance was limited to a common-sense understanding of common-sense principles. In this case, as in so many others, simplicity, reliability, and longevity go hand-in-hand.

Europe has numerous examples of tracker-action organs that are three hundred years old and more. The bottom line is that, aside from artistic considerations (and many if not most organists and builders tend to prefer trackers for artistic reasons), tracker action represents the wisest economy and should be chosen whenever and wherever it is possible to do so, especially for a small pipe organ.

I have alluded to organ placement in discussing the matter of key action, and shall now make a few observations about it. The precepts to follow are valid for any organ, tracker- or electric-action. However, they pertain most directly to one with tracker action, with pipework and keydesk in close proximity. Good placement can mean the difference between success and failure for any organ; in fact, fewer stops, properly placed, will be far more effective than many stops in an organ that has been poorly situated. In other words, a smaller, less costly instrument can do a far better job than a more expensive, larger one—if the smaller instrument is carefully placed.

The basics of good organ placement are not complicated. First, the organ's pipework must be physically within the sanctuary. Chambers (rooms located off the chancel, some even specifically designed and prepared by the architect and contractor for the organ) dramatically cut an instrument's effectiveness. The organ should stand totally within the room in which it is to be heard, with open

A well-placed pipe organ speaks directly down the length of a sanctuary, rather than from side chambers in a chancel. This encased instrument, a two-manual and pedal organ of thirty-two stops was manufactured by W. Zimmer & Sons, Charlotte, North Carolina, and installed in 1981 in the Ascension Lutheran Seminary, Philadelphia. Note the location of the keydesk.

space at the front, sides, top, and even back. Even with tracker action the keydesk can be reversed, so that the organist has his or her choir before, and the pipework in back, if that is advisable.

Second, the organ should be located on a narrow wall if the room is rectangular in shape, so that it speaks down the length of the sanctuary. It, and the choir, may be in a rear gallery, or in front, behind the pulpit or a free-standing altar or holy table. If such an arrangement is simply impracticable for the situation, then the organ *can* be located at the side of a chancel, with the keydesk reversed so that the organist can see and be seen by the choir; however, such an arrangement is a definite compromise.

Third, the organ should be housed in a free-standing resonant, sound-reflecting wood case. While the practice of displaying uncased pipes in the open is frequently followed, and is certainly far superior to burying them in chambers, the presence of a case, quite apart from the striking visual effect it provides, will blend and focus the tone, take the edge off any harshness, and provide clarity, buoyancy, and a sort of "halo" to the tone.

These principles are the time-tested ones by which the finest organs of the past and the present have been and are being built. The first two will not add to the cost of the instrument, but they enhance its musical effectiveness a good deal. Encased pipework may increase cost somewhat. All three principles should be adhered to rigorously, in the case of both trackers and electric-action instruments.

The pipe organ is certainly the most costly of the three types of church instruments that will be considered in this book. In general, a pipe organ will cost at least five times that of an equivalent size electronic organ. On the other hand, the pipe organ could well last ten times as long, with less overall maintenance cost. At the end of their respective periods, the electronic organ will almost certainly have to be replaced, whereas the pipe organ will be rebuildable at substantially less (a third to a half the figure may be about right) than an equivalent new organ would cost.

There will certainly be situations in which the high initial cost of a pipe organ will make it impracticable for a given church. I shall have more to say about costs and ways of saving as this book goes on. At this point, however, the idea of a pipe organ ought not to be dismissed as out of consideration for economic reasons. More than one church has discovered that a pipe organ was possible for the same amount as (or less than) an electronic.

5

Electronic Organs

The final paragraph of the last chapter notwithstanding, there are situations in which, for architectural, economic, or other reasons, an electronic organ may be the best choice; indeed, the only choice. Electronic instruments have made great strides in longevity and reliability, to say nothing of tone quality, over the past decade.

There are certain very real reasons, however, why the electronic organ has not quite managed to imitate the pipe organ. First, tones are generated by electronic equipment rather than by pipes. The actual vibrating medium, rather than dispersed individual pipes, is one of a set of speakers. Thus, a number of tones—notes of various stops—must share a single "resonator" or speaker, whereas in a pipe organ each tone has its own "speaker," the pipe that generates it.

Second, the "presence" and complexity of certain pipe tones, especially those of reed pipes, such as trumpets, simply cannot be captured by state-of-the-art electronic equipment at any kind of economic advantage over the cost of a pipe organ. To put it another way, anybody who knows the first thing about computer capabilities knows that the technology exists to surmount this drawback. In fact, it exists to surmount the drawback outlined in the last para graph. The problem is that the expense of doing so is such as to

This Saville Sovereign console has tilting stop and coupler tablets. Note the transposer to the right of the keyboards. It is manufactured by Saville Organs, Wichita, Kansas.

make the project impracticable. It would be cheaper, in fact, to build the original—a pipe organ—than to go to the expense of faithfully counterfeiting it.

Nevertheless, the electronic organ is a viable musical instrument, and its potential for church use should not be sold short. Whether or not it should be compared with a pipe organ is irrelevant—it will continue to be, no matter what. Many churches have been totally satisfied with their electronic organs, and do not hesitate to say so.

This chapter may sound more like a catalog of drawbacks rather than the kind of descriptive and explanatory essay that made up the chapter on pipe organs. There are several reasons for this. First, the principles on which an electronic organ operates, while they are not hard to grasp, especially for laymen who have had an interest in some aspect of electronics, radio, hi-fi, or computers, are not as easily described as are the principles on which a pipe organ operates. Second, electronic organs do not lend themselves to practical repairs by mechanically inclined laymen, as do pipe organs, especially trackers. If something goes wrong, and it does quite often in older electronic organs, then the trained technician must be called.

Stops are controlled by drawknobs on this Baldwin console. Tilting tablets control coupling functions. Note the toe pistons above the pedalboard. The manufacturer is the Baldwin Organ Company, Cincinnati, Ohio.

Finally, the nomenclature used in electronic organ stops, the grouping into divisions on manuals and pedal, and the general appearance of electronic organs—at least the quality instruments made for church use—are the same as those on a pipe organ. The organist's function is the same; the selection of stops is the same; and in general, any explanation of stops, manuals, etc., for an electronic organ would of necessity repeat needlessly what has already been said in the last chapter.

Certain disadvantages, in addition to the tonal ones discussed above, should be considered in weighing the low initial cost of an electronic as opposed to a pipe organ. The major one is longevity. Today's state-of-the-art bodes somewhat better for electronic organs functioning with minimal repairs for a bit longer than the ten-to-fifteen-year lifespan that used to be accorded them. Nevertheless, it must be kept in mind that whereas electronic organs require comparatively little maintenance early in their lives, they become very expensive to repair and keep operative as they get older.

Moreover, the same state-of-the-art pace that rendered last decade's—and last year's—model obsolete, will of necessity render this year's model obsolete within the next year or two. To put it another way, the "state-of-the-art" of electronics is still evolving; that of pipe organs is at its ultimate. A three-hundred-year-old pipe organ can easily be faithfully restored and rebuilt by any first-rate modern builder; a twenty-year old electronic organ can no more be rebuilt, at least economically, than a twenty-year-old television set, with which it shares so much in common.

Some electronic organs are manufactured specifically for use in homes. These ought definitely *not* to be considered for churches. Consider only the church organs of builders whose work is aimed at churches and serious organists, and is so recognized. There is, in truth, little to choose among them. All are proud of their products; all take special pains to provide the best possible components and workmanship; all have made careful studies of pipe-tone generation and electronic methods for duplicating it; all have made very successful installations in rather prestigious churches and concert halls.

Each makes every effort to distinguish its specific method of tone generation—digital as opposed to oscillators, for instance. I have played examples of each, and must confess that I find the musical superiority of one method of tone generation over another far from manifest. Digital generation and computerization is certainly promising; however, the problem of speaker sharing (among others) acts as a formidable equalizer or leveler. If, indeed, the basic tone quality of the sound generated by this or that subtly different method is to make a considerable impression, some means must be found whereby it can escape the bottleneck of speaker limitation; for, if indeed the tone generated is superior, what emerges from the speakers is not noticeably so.

Like a pipe organ, much of the success or failure of an electronic organ is determined by speaker placement. As in the placement of a pipe-organ case, the speakers should be situated in such a way as to command the length of the sanctuary.

Even more important, only the highest available quality speaker units should be accepted. If funds are limited in such a way that the choice must be made between a smaller organ with fewer stops but absolutely top-of-the-line speakers on the one hand, and a larger instrument with more stops, but with less elaborate speaker units on the other, opt unhesitatingly for the former. It is far better to procure an instrument two or three stops smaller and use the funds saved to invest in a speaker system two or three grades better than what would normally be had. The bargain does not involve volume;

Consoles for electronic organs are very similar to those for pipe organs and are built according to specifications adopted by the American Guild of Organists. The model shown, is manufactured by the Allen Organ Company, Macungie, Pennsylvania.

that may be had rather cheaply. What it does involve is cleanness and the "spread" that can be had only with a number of mounted speakers spreading the tonal speech over a wider area.

These "trade-offs" can be made fairly easily in planning a larger custom installation. Smaller instruments are "stock" models, mass-produced, and while there are varying degrees of "voicing" adjustments possible on them, they are, essentially, compromise instruments. They are intended to serve adequately—with minor adjustments here and there—in sanctuaries varying in size, shape, and liveliness, not to mention varied worship needs. It thus becomes very important to make up for inherent design compromises by upgrading speaker quality as much as possible.

Saying it again—because it is very important—in yet another way, effect economies in the size of the organ, i.e., the number of stops and not in the quality of the speakers.

It is also important with any organ, but especially with an electronic organ, that the committee, in considering a particular make and model, hear that instrument at work; not in a studio with a carefully controlled acoustical environment and often with especially good speaker equipment; and not in an *empty* church. If possible find an installation in an acoustic environment close to that of your own sanctuary. Hear the instrument support congregational hymns; hear it support the choir; hear it play preludes and postludes. Be especially attentive to any distortion at high dynamic levels, any unpleasant random noises, undertones or colors, any roughness in the tone, any thinning of the tone quality.

Remember, any electronic organ—even the old 1930s tube-types—could be made to sound well played softly and through adequate speakers. The strength and clarity needed for adequate congregational support *has* to be present. Otherwise, forget the instrument, no matter how many "pretty" effects in the soft and medium range it has; no matter how many stop combinations and special sounds it can make. When all is said and done, it will *not* do the job.

Also, beware of being sidetracked by assorted gadgets and gimmicks. Reputable salesmen for electronic organs for churches do not try to sell an instrument on the basis of useless rhythm sections, artificial reverberation units (which sound dreadful and do nothing for dead acoustics, claims to the contrary notwithstanding), and the like. One gadget that is really quite useful is a transposer. Many electronic organs are equipped with them. They permit a hymn to be played as written, but to sound a second, third, or more lower; a great boon for congregations who are discouraged by too many high notes.

One final note worthy of serious consideration: Many professional organists and church musicians simply will not accept a position that involves playing or working with an electronic organ. Depending on the supply of organists available for positions in your area—and no area has a surplus of good ones—and your long-range plans for growth in the quality and size of your parish music program, you may wish to weigh this factor and the subsequent ramifications of selecting an electronic organ, even a large and well-equipped one, rather than a more modest pipe organ.

6

Reed Organs

Only recently have some churches and organists in the United States awakened to the possibilities of reed organs as a viable option for the small and medium-sized church, especially a congregation on a limited budget. Partially, this is because reed organs have not been manufactured in this country for the past twenty-five years. Nevertheless, large numbers survive from the nearly one hundred years during which they were made in astonishingly large numbers for homes, schools, studios, chapels, and churches. Most of these instruments were "parlor" organs: the pump organs so familiar in the living rooms of two or more generations ago. A considerable number, however, are larger "chapel" and "church" models, many of them having two manuals and a pedal board. These are eminently adequate for use in many sanctuaries, even fairly large ones, if they are equipped with a sufficiently-sized blower (or rather, suction unit, for most American-made ones, in contrast to the European harmoniums, operate on the suction of air).

A number of concerns are actively restoring old reed organs. Replacement parts are readily available for components that wear out, and the mechanism by which the instruments work is reliable, long-lasting, and basically quite simple. The instruments scarcely ever need tuning. Thus there is comparatively little that can go wrong

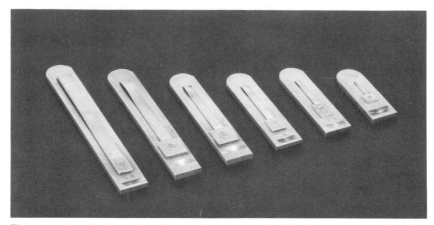

The sound-producing parts of a reed organ are vibrating brass tongues, riveted to brass blocks, over openings that are slightly larger than the tongues themselves. Suction causes the reed to vibrate within its opening. The block fits snugly into a grooved reed cell, but is easily removed by inserting a reed puller into the indentation at the base of the reed block. Note the curvature at the end of some of the reeds shown here, influencing the distinctive timbre of the reed. Reeds seldom require tuning, even over very long periods of time.

with a reed organ, and several "overhauls" of "unplayable" instruments have restored the playability within a short time simply by cleaning the reeds thoroughly.

A few of the shops alluded to in the last paragraph are actively considering the design and manufacture of large reed organs again, for the church market. The cost, given the expense of today's labor and the craftsmanship involved, will probably be a good deal higher than the cost of restoring an old one. As a rough estimate, the price for a new reed organ of two manuals and modern design will probably run about 10 to 15 percent of the cost of a two-manual pipe organ: a shade less than an electronic instrument of comparable size. Meanwhile, fully restored and renovated old reed organs of two manuals and pedal may be had at prices far, far lower: less even than the cost of a good spinet piano.

Naturally, the market in any second-hand item will fluctuate with the demand for that product and its availablility. Reed organs, although plentiful now, are obviously finite in number, and will doubtless increase in price over the next few years as more and more of them find permanent homes. It was not long ago that a second-hand tracker-action pipe organ could be had virtually for the taking, but there again, the supply was finite, and the costs for

LEFT: A Mason and Hamlin reed organ from the early 1900s, in use in the Hillside Congregational Church, Cornish, Maine. This instrument has a straight pedalboard. The pipes over the keydesk are for visual effect only. Most reed organ manufacturers offered the option of a "pipe top" for their larger "church" instruments. Reed organs such as this may be acquired at very low cost, restored economically, and placed in service in small and even medium-sized churches. RIGHT: A similar two-manual-and-pedal reed organ without the "pipe top." This one, with a radiating pedalboard, is in use in the Shapleigh Baptist Church, Shapleigh, Maine. The stoplist is almost the same as the Cornish instrument.

these restorable instruments have skyrocketed. There is no reason to suppose that the same thing will not eventually occur with reed organs. Nevertheless, even were they to become procurable only at a substantially higher price, reed organs would still be worthy of thorough investigation and careful consideration by the prudent organ committee.

Historically, reed organs have a long tradition of serving churches, large and small. European cathedrals, especially those in France and Germany, often have a harmonium—as European reed organs are called—in the choir loft, for accompanying daily devotions. Small churches in the United States and Canada often chose reed organs rather than very small pipe organs in the late nineteenth and early twentieth centuries, before the advent of electronics. Although electronic organs are ubiquitous in rural churches in the United States, their counterparts in Canada have largely retained their reed organs, seeing—in that sort of wisdom traditionally found in rural areas—no reason to replace what was doing a perfectly good job, simply because it had been doing so for many years and was therefore presumably "old."

Reed organs, as may be gathered from the foregoing, last as long, for all practical purposes, as mechanical-action pipe organs, probably because they share so much with them in simple principles of operation and mechanism. Moreover, such little things that do go wrong are comparatively easily repaired. Tunings last for years, if not decades. And finally, reed organs not only hold their value; they appreciate. A two-manual that could be had for $200 ten years ago, now may cost over $2,000, and will doubtless go higher in years ahead.

For our purposes, the parlor organ should not be considered, although it works on the same principle as its larger brothers and can, indeed, be pressured so as to fill a generous-sized auditorium. It will be more appropriate to turn to the various types of reed organs, marketed during their period of popularity, as "church" and "chapel" organs.

Reed organs function, as has been observed, on substantially the same principles as do pipe organs. The sound is generated by wind, in this case causing metal strips, called reeds, to vibrate. The dynamic level is governed by the amplitude of the vibration (which can be controlled either by bending the end of the reed or by increasing the vacuum). The tone color is governed by the shape of the reeds.

Nomenclature and pitch are the same, for the player's purposes, as on a pipe or electronic organ. The reed organ, however, in most cases has less capacity for variety, and herein lies its major drawback. Although the stop names may differ one from another, there is among them, in fact, a marked similarity.

Nevertheless, the reed organ is adequate to the demands of most churches. It is long-lived, reliable, and a distinct option, especially where funds and space are limited.

The reed organ may be an ideal "temporary" instrument in which to invest part of an organ fund while that fund is growing to the size where it will purchase a pipe organ, for instance. The reed organ, so employed, will appreciate in value, even as it is doing regular Sunday service.

7

Rebuilding an Old Organ

W hile a pipe organ might be the ideal, it is also the most expensive of the three types of instruments. That factor alone causes many committees quite early in the course of their deliberations to rule out the possibility of buying a pipe organ. It is viewed as an option beyond their congregation's fiscal capabilities. Such a decision is unfortunate because a large saving over the price of a new instrument can be effected by finding and restoring an old one; or, if a church is fortunate enough to have an old instrument that is restorable, of doing so.

Recycling is an option that should be explored thoroughly. It is a viable one both for new churches seeking to acquire their first instrument and for the church whose presently used organ appears to have passed beyond the stage of functional reliability. (Electronic organs, for the record, simply do not lend themselves to rebuilding or restoration any more than an old stereo does.)

No church that already owns a pipe organ should discard it without first calling in a qualified, disinterested person who is not affiliated with a builder of pipe organs or with a dealer in electronic instruments. After a reasonably careful but not especially lengthy examination, he or she should be able to ascertain whether or not the old instrument can be rebuilt or renovated into an adequate organ at a reasonable cost; and if not, what if any materials from it can be salvaged for incorporating into a new instrument. If the organ can be renovated, as is very frequently the case, the church will certainly save a good deal of money (enough to justify many times over the fee of the visiting expert), and end up with an organ that is far better than it could otherwise have afforded.

If the church's old organ is a tracker-action (mechanical) instrument, even if it is well over a century old, there is virtually no question that it can be restored for a fraction of the cost of a comparable new instrument (provided, of course, that it has not been vandalized seriously, or suffered water or fire damage, or sustained other than the ordinary wear, tear, and deterioration of time and hard use). Much to their subsequent regret, many churches have allowed themselves to be convinced otherwise by less-than-scrupulous organ salesmen. While one may extend such a victimized church a measure of sympathy and even a pinch of understanding, one should also learn from its sad blunder and take special care to avoid repeating it.

The church with an organ forty to seventy years old having pneumatic or electric (or electropneumatic) action, is somewhat less fortunate. Such an organ may well be salvageable. However, the expense of renovating the deteriorated mechanism by replacing disintegrated leather portions and superannuated electrical parts, added to the cost of the tonal changes that are almost unavoidable in the case of most instruments from that particularly unfortunate era in musical taste, can quickly add up to a generous amount. In fact, the total may well be considerably more than the sum necessary to restore a mechanical-action instrument a half-century or more older! The question of the viability and practicability of renovating or rebuilding an electropneumatic, electric, or tubular pneumatic organ (a type made for a brief period at the beginning of the present century) is one to be decided only after having secured the advice of a thoroughly competent disinterested individual.

If the church has no organ, or determines, after careful consideration and with competent counsel, that the instrument it has is not worth rebuilding, the committee should consider the option of purchasing an old tracker organ from some other church or institution. The instrument should be a tracker for the reasons outlined in the preceding paragraph. Also, factors such as reliability and longevity must be of paramount concern in any project involving a second- or third-hand organ, and mechanical action instruments, as

Originally built as a one-manual instrument by George Jardine & Son, New York City, 1874, for a Brooklyn Church, this organ was converted to a two-manual instrument by the same firm in 1893. Today it is installed in St. Mary's Church, Charleston, South Carolina. Relocation was arranged by the Organ Clearing House. Restoration and installation were carried out by Mann & Trupiano, New York, 1980.

Opus 1276 of Hook & Hastings, Boston, 1885, was originally built for the School of Music in Cleveland. Later it served a church on Cleveland's west side. Through the help of the Organ Clearing House it was dismantled, moved, restored, and reinstalled in 1980 in the Sacred Heart Church, Marlborough, New Hampshire. Parish volunteers stripped and refinished the oak case. Tonal revisions were made by Mann & Trupiano, New York.

observed earlier, are extremely long-lived and reliable. (The option of the refurbished second-hand reed organ should come to mind here for those readers whose parishes are small—or even not so small—and able to raise a very limited amount for the organ.)

Old organs become available regularly because of church closings and mergers. The main source for churches seeking such instruments is a non-profit, one-man operation which has saved many such instruments from being wrecked or vandalized while at the same time finding new homes for them in congregations who badly want fine organs but simply cannot afford the cost of a new pipe organ. The Organ Clearing House, Harrisville, New Hampshire, a labor of love run by a former high-school English teacher, Alan M. Laufman, has relocated literally hundreds of old pipe and reed organs to the unalloyed delight and significant financial saving of the recipient churches.

Once an old organ has been located and purchased, and removed from its former home, it usually needs mechanical refurbishing, tonal alteration, and perhaps visual reconstruction, so as to fit better with the decor of its new surroundings. Assuming that the work is properly done by a builder experienced in renovating old American organs, the resulting instrument will be the equal of a new organ costing half-again to twice as much, and will serve in its new home for a century or more.

Occasionally an organ is in good enough condition to warrant its simply being set up in its new home. St. Anne's Church, Lowell, Massachusetts, my own parish, has in its chapel a small single-manual organ built in 1881 by the New York maker, Hilborne L. Roosevelt, for a small church in Alexandria Bay, New York. The organ was subsequently moved to a church in Evans Mills, New York. When the Evans Mills church closed, the organ was rescued from the wreckers and placed in storage. Over a year later it was purchased by the vestry of St. Anne's and found to be mechanically and tonally sound. With only a careful cleaning it was set up in the chapel. The instrument did require cosmetic work: the removal of

This organ in the Grace Episcopal Church, Amherst, Massachusetts, contains some recycled parts of an organ built by John G. Marklove in 1883, relocated through the Organ Clearing House. Also included are older pipes, many from an earlier electro-pneumatic instrument in the church, all suitably revoiced. The organ has two manuals and pedal, with mechanical key action throughout. The organ was built and installed by the Stuart Organ Company, Aldenville, Massachusetts.

water spots on the display pipes, four new key ivories, one new stop-knob label, and a few other like items. However, it was eminently playable and usable—indeed, regularly used—after having simply been set up. Another church in a nearby town purchased and transported a larger two-manual organ from Pennsylvania, set it up, and played it the next Sunday. The total cost in both cases was but a fraction of what an electronic would have cost: and not much more than the cost of a reconditioned reed organ.

Such instruments, requiring little or no work are not the usual case, of course. The ultimate cost of an organ recycling project will depend on a number of factors, such as the availability of an organ that will fit the shape and size of the space set aside for it in its new home, the amount of tonal revision necessary or desired, and the amount of volunteer help willing and able to assist in the nontechnical tasks such as dismantling, moving, and re-erecting the organ.

The option of a recycled organ is real; both musically and economically viable. Procuring, restoring, and installing a recycled organ can be the kind of "self-reliant" project that knits together men and women of a congregation in the common desire to have a really fine organ and the opportunity to have a "hands-on" part in providing that single largest piece of worship furnishing for their church. This fringe benefit alone commends the project as one worthy of a lively and growing church. The ramifications of a recycling project will be discussed in a later chapter.

8

Maintenance Considerations

A major concern of any committee contemplating the purchase of an organ should be service and maintenance costs. Salesmen for some electronic instruments tend to stress the contrast between a pipe organ's need for periodic maintenance and regular tuning and their own product's freedom from such servicing requirements. This is, strictly speaking, not entirely so. Thus, it is the purpose of this chapter to lay down some practical guidelines for planning servicing and maintenance costs for the various types of instruments, based not on claims but rather on performance records.

The most reliable, long-lasting, and maintenance-free instrument, in the long run, is without a doubt the tracker-action pipe organ. Its principle of operation is simple, there is little that can malfunction, and what does can be easily understood and repaired. Like all pipe organs, it requires tuning about twice a year. At the time the tuning is done, minor maintenance and servicing may also be done. The service contract on a small one- or two-manual organ should be quite reasonable, even from the most expensive technician. A good rule-of-thumb is that from 1 to 2 percent of the cost of an organ, budgeted each year into a "revolving" fund, will take care not only of maintenance but also any major repairs that become necessary—including fairly large-scale projects that may become advisable one hundred years down the line.

In the long run, a tracker-action pipe organ is most reliable and relatively maintenance-free. However, as in all pipe organs, periodic tuning and minor servicing are
necessary. Shown here is the small, one-manual and pedal organ of the Dilworth
Lutheran Church, Dilworth, Minnesota. Consisting of eight ranks and six stops, this
tracker-action pipe organ requires little floor space. It was designed, built, and installed by the Johnson Organ Company, Fargo, North Dakota.

The tracker organ's smaller cousin, the reed organ, has a comparable degree of reliability and longevity, again because its principle of operation is simple, its mechanism is reliable, and much of what can go wrong with it—and that is comparatively little—can be repaired by a layman. A reed organ needs tuning rarely, if ever. Many reed instruments that have not been tuned since they left the shop, fifty, seventy-five, and even a hundred years ago are still playing acceptably today. A dead note is usually caused by dirt. Removal of the reed and cleaning it is a simple operation. Felts, leather, and rubberized cloth deteriorate over a long period of time; however, these parts are easily obtainable, even by the amateur, from the many piano tuners' supply houses. There are many amateur "parlor" organ restorers whose skill is readily adaptable to the needs of a larger reed organ—in fact, your church may well have one or two in the congregation.

In the cases both of reed and of pipe organs (tracker and electric), the motor powering the blower or suction unit must be checked regularly, like any other electric motor.

Electric and electropneumatic pipe organs require somewhat more maintenance, at least beyond the twentieth to twenty-fifth year. Depending on the chemical content of the atmosphere in the area, leathers will begin to fail in from twenty to fifty years. Releathering is quite expensive. Given inflation, I will avoid quoting specific prices, knowing that any figure valid today will almost certainly be invalid a year from now; however, it is fair to say that a releathering, competently done, will cost up to 20 percent of the price of a comparable new instrument at the time the job is done. If it would cost about $100,000 in 1983 dollars to replace a given instrument with a modern one of the same size, releathering the instrument can be expected to cost about $20,000, done by a competent firm in a proper manner. Some research has gone into developing synthetic materials to replace the lambskin used on pneumatics; however, such synthetics fail either to hold their flexibility over the requisite long periods of time under a variety of temperatures and humidity conditions, or—and this is a nagging problem—to bond properly with the wood through the use of appropriate adhesives. It may well be that a synthetic material is just around the corner that will render properly tanned leather obsolete in electropneumatic organ mechanisms. As of this writing, there is no thoroughly reliable sub-

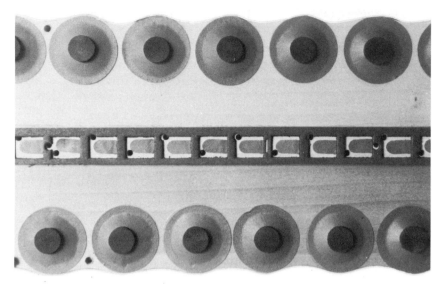

The life expectancy of leather used in an electro-pneumatic-action organ may vary with atmospheric conditions. Properly tanned and treated leathers (some are treated with silicone) may last for forty or fifty years, however this is usually considered their maximum life. Shown here are pouch boards for an electro-pneumatic pipe organ.

stitute. And since leathers are perishable, large releathering projects are endemic to electropneumatic organ mechanisms.

Permanent magnetizing is also a product of age, especially in all-electric actions utilizing few or no leather pneumatics. Here again, the cost for repair is high.

For electric and electro-pneumatic organs, the same one-or two-visits-a-year maintenance schedule and twice-a-year tuning schedule is necessary. Because of the nature of the mechanism, a service contract will probably be somewhat higher than on an equivalent-size tracker.

It is appropriate here to dispell the prevailing misconception among laymen *and organists,* that the organ suffers if the heat is turned down in the church between services during the winter. That simply is not so. In fact, the exact opposite is true. Far more pipe organs of all types have been irreversibly damaged by dry central heat. Such heat can draw the moisture out of the wood, causing it to warp and crack, necessitating expensive repairs. If at all possible, the church should *not* be heated during the week in the winter (summer's heat, after all, is a moist heat in most places). If for some reason, continuous heating is necessary, it is essential that controlled humidification equipment be installed to preserve the organ (as well as any fine pieces of wood furnishings in the church!). But by far, the best course of action is to turn the heat down as far as possible. Organs in Europe and America, after all, have thrived for decades and centuries without central heating. One of the saddest sights is to go into an old church with an old organ, that has recently begun to heat the church sanctuary continuously, and to discover that the organ, which has survived dozens of heatless winters, is being—or has been—dried out almost to the point of irreparable damage by the new policy. Probably the greatest beneficiaries of the recent high fuel prices will be the organs in churches that can no longer afford to keep the heat up during the week.

This misconception about heat being necessary for an organ doubtless grows out of the observed phenomenon of the reed ranks going out of tune as the temperature drops. In fact, it is not the reeds that are temperature sensitive, but rather the other ranks of pipes. What makes the reeds seem so obvious is that the *rest* of the organ slips in pitch due to the expansion or contraction of the metal pipes caused by the temperature change (wood pipes tend to "draw" into tune), so that the flue ranks, although they are out of tune, are uniformly out of tune, and so in-tune with each other. The reeds, which have remained at pitch, sound awry.

Regardless of the foregoing phenomenon, as soon as the heat returns to the temperature it was when the instrument was tuned— say, for a Sunday morning service, for example—the organ will be found to have "moved" back into tune again.

Electronic organs are indeed largely free of service for the first few years of their lives. However, after five to ten years components will begin to give trouble regularly, first one, then another, sometimes failing suddenly and without warning, and often requiring numerous visits, especially from the age of about twelve or fifteen years on, each at a substantial "minimum" fee for labor, in addition to whatever parts are necessary (not unlike the visit of the TV repairman, for example). Claims to the contrary notwithstanding, older electronic organs can and often do develop tuning problems, in addition to the uniquely electronic problems of random static and distortion. The one-hundred-year old third-hand tracker in St. Anne's chapel replaced a twenty-year-old electronic instrument, the finest available at the time of its purchase. It became unusable because of the distortion.

In a nutshell, the longevity is highest—one hundred years or more—and servicing over the long term lowest, with a tracker-action pipe organ. This is a generally conceded matter of fact, not of opinion, and borne out by the record. Longevity is somewhat less— about forty years before major work is necessary—and service somewhat higher, for an electric- or electropneumatic-action pipe organ. Servicing in the long run is highest and longevity least on electronic organs. Reed organ longevity and maintenance costs are negligible concerns.

The intent of the above is not to dissuade a committee from purchasing anything but a tracker-action pipe organ (even though the facts, baldly stated, militate for that course). Indeed, many churches simply cannot afford such an instrument, even in a recycling project; or their sanctuary cannot accommodate a pipe organ for architectural or structural reasons. Rather, its intent is to clarify the servicing and longevity aspects of the various types of organs so that each committee can balance all the factors adequately as it deliberates the best choice for its unique situation.

9

The Role of the Consultant

A large church about to embark on an organ project will engage a consultant. Does your church need one? The purpose of this book, after all, is to fill in some of the gaps in your committee's organ knowledge, to save the church from making a serious and costly error because of lack of information. Is that not fulfilling the role of the consultant? The answer is yes and no. This book, as stated at the beginning, will not make an organ expert of anybody. Hopefully, it will make for an adequately informed lay committee. It may save many, if not most churches, the cost of a consultant from the beginning to the end of the organ process. In the case of a modest recycling project, or the purchase of a reed organ, it might satisfy the need for semitechnical information that would have prompted the committee to seek out a knowledgeable person's advice.

Nevertheless, it is a good idea to have somebody who is knowledgeable about organ design and construction, and about church music, available to answer questions when they arise and even to discuss the church's needs with the builder as the designs for the organ are being drawn up. We have already seen how a qualified person must be retained when a committee is attempting to determine whether or not an old organ is worth salvaging. And a consultant can ease many of the problems in determining the needs of the parish and deciding on the proper design and builder to execute it. A consultant can also serve to interpret the concerns of the church to the builder, and those of the builder to the church at certain times.

It should be stated emphatically, however, that *all* major builders and the overwhelming majority of smaller ones (who have, by the way, stayed that way to maintain what they feel strongly is a degree of personal quality that can be had only in a shop with a few highly skilled artisans working together on all facets of an organ) are characterized by integrity and pride in what they do. No consultant is ever needed to supervise an installation, and no consultant should attempt to override a builder to insist on his or her particular ideas against the experience and best advice of the builder. A consultant who does so is a definite danger to the success, quality, and continued good-will of the project. A builder who requires the supervision of a consultant as "clerk-of-the-works" ought not to have been selected to do the job in the first place. Most consultants will withdraw from a project if the builder chosen, against prior advice, must be supervised in order to get first-class work.

The real role of the consultant, regardless of the misconceptions held by some, is to act neither as an "architect" nor as a "clerk-of-the-works" to see that the builder is doing a proper job. Rather, the consultant has three major functions.

First, he or she should utilize a combination of expertise in organ design and construction on one hand, and in church music and worship needs on the other, to assist the laypersons of the organ committee to define for themselves just what it is they will want and need from the organ they choose to fill worship requirements.

Second, the consultant should assist the committee in determining the builder or builders best able to provide the type of organ decided on, within budgetary and other limitations. He or she should then work with the builder who is subsequently chosen to do the work—as a church musician, *not* an "architect"—to develop the best specifications possible within the limitations laid down. Two points should be mentioned here. First, many organ builders, especially smaller ones, began as church musicians and a number are still active as such. Accordingly, such a builder will not be unaware of, but rather sympathetic to, worship needs. Second, never should the consultant be expected or allowed to determine mixture breaks, pipe scales, or other technical data, except in conjunction and by agreement with the builder. The consultant, however, *should* be given the right and responsibility of approving the final acceptance of the instrument, for he or she is, after all, the church's representative. Any changes in design should be made by the builder and consultant together.

The third and final duty of the consultant is the most difficult and yet the most important. He or she must act as a "go-between" to explain to the church why it must, for example, pay a third of the price upon signing the contract and subsequent installments at intervals before the organ is finished. The consultant must explain that the builder is making large initial material outlays and therefore would otherwise have an immense cash flow problem, were his clients to pay him cash-on-delivery; or why many—indeed, virtually all—builders fall behind on the intended delivery date; why the builder becomes testy and abnormally (at least to the average church member) fussy about details that seem so minor. (The church member forgets that it is the builder's name that goes on the organ for posterity and potential future clients to see.) The consultant reassures the committee, explains any changes in the original specifications, and generally becomes the "whipping boy" for both builder and committee.

From my own personal experience, I can testify ardently that nobody is happier and more relieved when an organ is finished, signed off, and the last payment made, than is the consultant.

It is far less important that a consultant be a thorough-going expert in organs, organ design, and even organ literature—still less, a local organist of some celebrity—than that he or she be a sensitive and experienced church musician with some knowledge of organ design and construction, a sympathetic, diplomatic, patient, and understanding person, preferably with nerves of iron and a sense of humor, and always taking assurance in the knowledge that once the organ is in, the congregation and committee will congratulate one another, the consultant, and the builder, and forget the trials and grilling through which it put its consultant as he or she ricocheted back and forth between committee and builder.

A consultant is hired by the church and ethically receives no remuneration for any reason from the builder. The church which the consultant represents pays his or her fee, ranging from a shamefully low honorarium to an hourly scale up to a maximum of a certain percentage of the contract price (depending on the reputation of the individual, and often his or her firmness). Compensation for the consultant should be agreed on, as with any professional, early in the process.

Generally, in the case of an organ consultant (as with anything else) the church will get what it pays for. Anything up to about 5 percent of the contract price is in line with proper remuneration, unless the job requires extraordinarily careful planning because of the size of the installation, or distinctive acoustical problems, in which case, the cost of a suitably qualified person may run slightly higher.

The church committee may find itself slightly surprised that its consultant and the builder selected seem to be rather friendly. It should rest assured that this cordiality is not a sign of a collusion. Most consultants who have had any experience have worked with or know personally most of the organ builders in a given area; there are, after all, not that many in the business. Neither builder nor consultant, when one stops to think about it, ought to view the other as an adversary, nor should the committee so view them, or itself.

To sum up, the consultant is the church's representative. His or her job is to see that the committee receives the advice it needs to make the best possible decisions at each and every stage of the project; to interpret the concerns of the committee to the builder, when necessary; and to interpret the concerns of the builder to the committee. Sadly, he or she is sometimes obstructed in his or her efforts to cooperate with the builder to provide the church with the best possible organ for its money by well-meaning stubbornness on the part of some committee members. Rarely is the intransigence of the builder a problem, by the way. Thus, for the sake of their reputation, to say nothing of their sanity, most consultants reserve the right to withdraw from a project at any time for good and appropriate reason.

As we move through the steps of an organ plan and purchase later in this book, more will be said, much by way of emphasis, about consultants and their use. For now, it is sufficient to say that carefully chosen, fairly compensated, and respectfully listened to, a consultant can be indispensable to both church and builder, not only in the area of the actual ongoing work, but also in the preservation of mutual respect and a good working relationship.

10

Summary of Pertinent Factors

At this point, we have covered the general information that every committee member should have at his or her command before beginning deliberations on the proper organ for his or her church. In the chapters to come, we shall walk through a procedure for procuring a church organ, look at some specific examples of instruments, and in general, apply the principles laid out to this point.

First, however, it may be of some assistance to the reader to summarize the information contained in the foregoing chapters, so as to facilitate a fairly quick comparison and consideration of the options open to the church organ committee. There may be some repetition; however, it is there for emphasis.

The pipe organ is generally conceded to be the best choice for a church—liturgically, artistically, and in terms of longevity. A mechanical or tracker-action pipe organ has a life expectancy literally measurable in centuries. An electropneumatic- or electric-action organ will last decades before major restorative work will be required. Maintenance, together with any such restoration as may become necessary after the years of trouble-free service that may be expected, will amortize to about 1 to 2 percent of the organ's price (new), per year. In the case of an electric or electropneumatic pipe organ, the percentage will on the average be somewhat higher because of the mechanism's somewhat shorter life expectancy.

The first disadvantage of tracker action as opposed to electric or electro-pneumatic-action organs is that it requires a sufficient and properly shaped space for pipework and keydesk, which must be in close proximity to each other, since the linkage is mechanical. Electric-action instruments, by contrast, accomplish connections with cables, and accordingly may be divided so as to fit in available and sometimes oddly-shaped spaces.

A pipe organ, however, will not sound as well as it might unless it is properly situated, in a proper case in the sanctuary, rather than in chambers, speaking through grills, no matter how widely open the grills are. Thus, the particular "discipline" imposed by the engineering problems in tracker action actually acts to the advantage of the organ, by compelling its placement and physical layout to be in the best interests of its sound, and the limitations are therefore all to the good, as far as musical results are concerned.

The second disadvantage of the tracker organ is its comparative initial expense and the waiting period necessary between the time it is ordered and the time it is actually delivered and set up. Most tracker builders are small "custom" shops with fewer than a dozen craftsmen and apprentices. There are few if any opportunities to save time or labor by "mass production" methods.

On the other hand, however, the greater life-expectancy of a tracker organ mitigates heavily both its initial cost and the waiting period.

Nevertheless, if initial cost is a formidable barrier, yet what is really wanted is a tracker, the option of a "recycled" old tracker may provide the ideal solution.

Builders of electric- electropneumatic-action organs are on the whole large and well-established firms with solidly deserved reputations. They meet frequently with different situations and problems in regard to acoustics, architecture, placement, and worship needs. Their instruments are usually thoroughly musical, well made, and excellent choices in those not infrequently encountered situations that simply do not lend themselves to the installation of a tracker.

It is fair to say that most churches purchasing new pipe organs do *not* select trackers for a variety of reasons: economic, architec-

Almost all tracker-action instruments being built today are free-standing organs. Rosales Organ Builders, Upland, California, designed, built, and installed this instrument in Saint Anthony's Roman Catholic Church, Upland.

tural, and even liturgical. Thus, an organ committee which, having considered carefully the plusses and minuses of each option, chooses to contract with an established maker of electric- or electropneumatic-action organs for an instrument, need have no fear of the suitability of the resulting instrument for its needs. It is, of course, important to reiterate that the builder chosen be a reputable firm with several successful installations to its credit.

For the small church whose budget simply will not allow for a pipe organ, the reed organ provides a correspondingly reliable and long-lasting choice, especially if the sanctuary is of small to moderate size. While reed organs are no longer made in this country, numerous large one- and two-manual reed organs made around the turn of the century survive in excellent condition. Several are available at any given time from restorers who purchase them from churches, chapels, and homes that no longer have need for them, recondition them, and resell them at surprisingly modest prices.

In addition to its reliability, longevity, simplicity of operation, and ease of repair, the reed organ's main advantages are its modest space requirements—comparable to those of a small electronic—and its cost: far less than the least expensive practicable electronic. Moreover, reed organs hold or increase their value, and thus make an ideal investment for the small church seeking to build up an organ fund for a future purchase, yet still in need of an instrument for Sunday morning worship. Finally, reed organs function for years on end with neither servicing nor tuning.

The disadvantage of a reed organ lies in its limited tonal variety. While it is capable of considerable dynamic range, assuming that the blower (or suction unit) is the proper one for the size of the building, the tone-producing portions—the reeds themselves—are capable of but a very modest range of tonal colors. As a matter of interest, European reed organs use forced wind rather than suction, and this design provides for greater variety. New reed organs, if built in America once again will almost certainly be forced wind, rather than suction; unfortunately they will be far more expensive than older reconditioned suction ones. Even then, it is doubtful that their cost will exceed that of a modest electronic, let alone approach that of a new pipe organ.

An electronic organ has numerous advantages: the convenience of simply wheeling it to its place in the sanctuary, plugging it in, and playing it; the comparatively low initial price for which one

The choice of an electro-pneumatic instrument usually gives greater flexibility in design and placement. Note how the design of this encased electro-pneumatic organ was influenced by its location in the sanctuary. It was manufactured by the Reuter Organ Company, Lawrence, Kansas.

may be had (compared to a pipe organ of the same size); and the ease with which it may be acquired. Except for certain large custom designs, the wait for an electronic organ seldom exceeds more than a few days or a week. Finally, it can be made to function adequately in a variety of acoustical and architectural environments, although, like a pipe organ, it is at its best when its speakers have the length of the room to speak down.

It is most important—and this bears repeating—that the largest and best equipped electronic organ will fail, unless its tone is fed through a speaker system of proper design and sufficient quality. Far, far better that the next smaller model be chosen, that "echo" speakers at the rear of the sanctuary be dispensed with, rather than that any compromise be made in the main battery of speakers that

This organ generates its tones through a combination of electronics and traditional organ pipes. An adjustable tuning control helps overcome tuning problems caused by changing temperatures. Shown here is the Classic Series 205 built by the Rodgers Organ Company, Hillsboro, Oregon.

support congregational singing. An electronic organ can sound its best—just as in the case of a fine stereo sound system—only through the best procurable speaker components the maker offers with the model. The company itself will always equip its demonstration models with top-of-the-line speakers. On no account should a church attempt to effect a saving by stinting funds in the speaker units.

Disadvantages of the electronic organ should be recognized. Many organists simply will not play them and churches with electronic organs often find it harder to engage a competent musician. Industry advertising notwithstanding, electronic organs *do* require servicing and even tuning, especially after they are ten or fifteen years old. The cost of such work is sometimes quite high, and the state of the art may be expected to have advanced sufficiently to make the components of a decade-old electronic organ in need of replacement parts as obsolete as those of a decade-old television set.

The top makers, those whose intended clientele is institutional— churches, schools, and serious organists, as distinct from recreational home "fun machines"—maintain replacement parts for organs long since out of production. Nevertheless, the extensive renovation or rebuilding of an electronic organ after its twenty-year-or-so life expectancy has passed is for all practical purposes not cost effective, except in the case of the largest special custom models, where the expense may be justified.

Constant advances in electronics represent a two-edged sword. Whereas a pipe organ or a reed organ may be obtained with the confidence that the art whereby it was built is a mature one, and not susceptible to radical, or even moderate, change, an electronic organ—like other electronic devices, from wrist watches to weapons systems—can promise no such stability. The organ a church buys today, therefore, is a good deal more advanced than last year's model. But next year's model will represent a similarly dramatic advance over this year's.

These, in a nutshell, are the options. No prices have been given, as has been remarked, because they fluctuate over the period of years a book such as this should be able to serve church committees. For rough reference, however, an electronic organ will cost about 10 to 15 percent of the amount for a tracker with approximately the same number of stops, and 15 to 20 percent the amount for an electric or electropneumatic pipe organ of the same size. A "recycled" old tracker organ will cost one-third to one-half the price of a new tracker organ of the same size, and if it needs no restorative mechanical or tonal work, considerably less (although it is wise to bear in mind that the laws of supply and demand are and will continue forcing the prices asked and paid for salvageable old tracker organs upward). A "recycled" reed organ will cost about 10 to 20 percent of a similar-sized electronic instrument. New reed organs, if and when they are built, will probably cost about the same as an electronic organ. The best value, dollar for dollar, for a small church on a very limited budget, is without doubt a reed organ.

These relative costs are, of course, approximate, even as of this writing. Moreover, they represent an initial cost, to be amortized over the anticipated useful life of the instrument: at least one hundred years for a tracker or reed organ; forty years for an electric or electropneumatic pipe organ; and twenty years with no serious prospect of salvage for rebuilding for an electronic.

11

Weighing the Options

In the chapters to follow, we shall proceed systematically through the process of selecting and acquiring an organ. Because the procedure is considerably more involved, and therefore more appropriate for illustrating the various steps and decisions for a pipe organ than for a reed or electronic organ, our hypothetical instrument will be a pipe organ. Were the committee, however, to decide on an electronic organ, having gone through the preliminary considerations to be described, it would simply contact the half-dozen or so makers of church electronics, or their local representatives, arrange to hear the instruments of each maker in a Sunday morning service, subtract from the available money the amount necessary to procure the best possible speaker units, and then select the model of their choice consistent with the funds remaining. Advertising to the contrary notwithstanding, there is a remarkable similarity between the major makers in terms of quality and reliability, and no committee, once having determined to go the route of an electronic organ, need agonize over getting a brand of "prestige" electronic instrument and then discover too late that it had not gotten as much for its money as it would have with another "prestige" brand. Given the limitations of electronic organs, already discussed in full, no committee need fear getting an "inferior" instrument, as long as it stays with a recognized maker.

Always remember, with makers of both pipe and electronic organs, future business depends, above all, on consistently successful work. All builders are keenly aware that few professional groups communicate so closely among themselves as do the clergy and organists, and a single poor installation can kill prospective purchases in a whole city or geographical area. Thus makers and builders have very urgent vested interests in making their instruments and installations as satisfactory as is humanly possible.

Similarly, if after a review of the situation and the budget, a reed organ is decided on, the purchase and installation procedure is quite uncomplicated, and the Wednesday night decision of an organ committee could possibly result in the organ's being ready to play the very next Sunday.

A committee's initial decision must be whether or not the present organ in the church, if there is one, is worth rebuilding, and if not, which parts from it can be salvaged for use in a new organ. At this specific stage, a competent disinterested person must be called in and asked to examine the organ and prepare a report for the committee. If funds allow, the committee may choose to ask two or even three people to prepare reports independently. I have been asked to prepare several such reports, in some cases without knowing that the committee had commissioned a similar report from another consultant. Two individuals may well disagree on particulars; however, if both are competent, they should arrive at the same conclusion as to whether or not the old organ is salvageable.

A builder's representative may later wish to examine the old organ, and may recommend less use of old materials. His recommendation, however, will often be based on what he knows to be his company's preference in the matter of using old chests, pipework, etc., and should not be viewed as a dispassionate and evenhanded opinion. Moreover, the committee will soon discover that the recommendations of builders' representatives are not necessarily consistent one with another.

As a general rule, a tracker-action organ, no matter how old, is restorable, unless it has suffered serious water or fire damage or has been particularly viciously vandalized. An old electronic organ, it scarcely needs be said, is not. In between, there is much room for experienced discretion, but no room for inexperienced opinion. The committee must make sure that whoever is to make the final recommendation knows what to look for, what constructional pitfalls there are, and what the costs of the restorations of the various parts will be. Some of these items will be discussed in the next chapter, concerned with "recycling" old organs. The decision is a complex one, and it cannot be made confidently by the committee of laypersons, unassisted.

Nor in selecting the individual to make the examination, should the committee assume that a local professional organist—even one with a graduate degree in church music, serving a large and important church in the area—can necessarily be counted on to possess the requisite knowledge. Assuming that a person who plays the organ well is also competent to pass on matters of organ building is roughly equivalent to assuming that the person who operates a computer well is competent to design or build one. He or she *may* be, of course; but the chances of it, no other evidence being present, are not very likely. Most organists will be quite honest about the depth, or lack thereof, of their knowledge of organ design and construction, so the committee need not worry overly much about being led astray by a well-meaning but fumbling individual. Nevertheless, it should ask a prospective advisor quite clearly if he or she understands just what it is that is expected and needed, and satisfy itself that information can and will be delivered with competence and accuracy.

If it is determined after careful examination that the old organ cannot be salvaged—or if there is no old organ—the committee proceeds to the next step: to consider its options as outlined above. If the old organ is rebuildable, the procedures described in the next chapter on "recycling" will apply as much to it as to an old organ obtained elsewhere.

Next the determination must be made on the basis of funds available and room, whether or not a recycled pipe organ is practicable. If *any* pipe organ is practicable, a recycled one will almost certainly be. Obviously, since the cost of the older instrument will be less than a new one, money is not a consideration. Similarly, if there is a commonly shaped space such as to admit the installation of a new organ of some depth, an old organ of as much depth may be installed as well.

Odd-shaped spaces present the main obstacles to the acquisition and employment of an old organ. I acted as consultant recently on an organ for a Catholic church which was to go in the rear gallery. Because the central window could not be blocked, and because the

Acquisition of an older tracker-action instrument is sometimes a limited option because of space restrictions. An organ consultant can give valuable assistance in matching an organ with the space available. This organ in St. Andrew's Church, Marblehead, Massachusetts, a recycled instrument from the nineteenth century, neatly fits the space available. The Kinzey-Angerstein Organ Company, Wrentham, Massachusetts, rebuilt the organ.

door to the belfry was on the right (as one faced the rear of the church), the only available space for the organ was in the gallery to the left of the window. This meant that the longer pipes (the basses) would have to be to the organist's *right*; in other words, a mechanical "roller" board would be necessary to transfer the key actions from the left to the pipes at the right. Certainly old trackers were so built upon occasion; however, they are not in plentiful supply these days, and the chance of finding one that fit this extraordinary situation was less than likely. Accordingly, since the parish had chosen to have a tracker and was able to fund the project, a new organ was designed.

In yet another situation, a not uncommon one, the space left in the choirloft was but eleven feet high. Even an old single-manual such as the Roosevelt in St. Anne's chapel, described earlier, requires more height than that. The speaking length of an open 8' pipe, after all, does not include the foot-and-a-half of pipe-foot below the mouth, the chest, and the action mechanism underneath it. In short, an old organ was simply impossible to fit in. Accordingly, a new one-manual, with a stopped 8' stop (therefore a pipe only half as long) had to be ordered.

In another situation the space provided for the organ was nearly thirty feet in height, but scarcely six feet square in floor area, necessitating that the manual divisions be one over the other. Now this was not a problem; in fact it is the classic European way of designing organs. American nineteenth-century instruments, however, are laid out for the most part on a single level with one manual division behind the other. The end result in this case, again, had to be a new organ.

Bear in mind that it is certainly possible to buy an old organ and redesign and re-engineer it so as to make it fit with a wrong-way roof line, or a low ceiling, or a small floor space; however, the cost of that sort of major reconstruction often ends up being as much or even more than what an instrument would have cost new.

At the stage of dealing with considerations such as these, the consultant can be invaluable. Presumably, the individual who evaluated the old organ, or somebody like him or her, will be available to assist in making these hard decisions. At this point, however, proper remuneration should be agreed on for his or her services. That remuneration will, of course, vary according to his or her experience, the amount of work, and the time and travel involved. Some consultants charge by the day or portion thereof, up to a fixed percentage of the final contract price. If the consultant is a recitalist, he may be asked to play the dedication program; however, the fee for this concert is usually over and above the consulting fees. Normally, the final fixing of a fee, if it is up to 2, 3, or 5 percent of the contract price, indicates his willingness to serve, and the church's willingness for him to serve, right through the final acceptance of the instrument.

It bears repeating, unfortunately, that a consultant may retain the hourly figure as a basis—at least initially—against the possibility that a church might ignore advice on a major item, such as the choice of a reputable builder (forgetting that the consultant is on *their* side) and persists in following what the consultant is convinced will result in severe detriment to the final result. In such a situation, after all arguments have proved futile, and the consultant feels he or she can no longer have his or her name associated with the project in good conscience, he or she should be able to withdraw from the situation and bill his or her time to date. Such a situation occurs but rarely; nevertheless, it has been known to happen. A consultant's name, just as that of a builder, can suffer harm from a poor installation with which he or she is associated. Hence, the "escape clause." Keep firmly in mind that if a consultant who has been carefully chosen, and who has the confidence of the committee, is concerned enough about a course of action to resign from the situation, the members of that committee would be well advised to heed his warnings and proceed with extreme caution. You ignore your own expert, after all, only at your extreme peril!

We now proceed to the options individually, and in order. Assuming that an old tracker has been procured (or, as stated above, already is owned by the church), decisions must be made as to who will do the work and what is to be done. The following chapter details the procedure to be followed in acquiring an old tracker, as well as renovating or rebuilding it.

12

The Process
of Recycling

Unless the church has its own organ, it will have to obtain one. There is an old recipe for rabbit stew that begins, "First, catch a rabbit. . . ." The only thoroughly dependable source, in my experience, for locating an available old pipe organ, is the Organ Clearing House, P.O. Box 104, Harrisville, New Hampshire 03450. (Inquiries should be accompanied by $2.50 in stamps for return postage).

Certain difficulties are attached to acquiring such an instrument, some of which may cause a church to alter its normal mode of business temporarily. Foremost is the problem of time. Not every organ available at a given time is suitable for every church seeking an instrument. One requiring twenty feet of height, for instance, is inappropriate for a sanctuary with fifteen-foot ceilings, and although the instrument could be altered to fit, the expense involved in doing so really defeats the purpose.

Similarly, an available organ may be located so far away as to make the cost of transportation prohibitive. Or, another available instrument, although fundamentally sound, may require extensive repairs, the cost of which will exceed the church's budget. Or an instrument's original voicing may be too loud or soft for the room, and the scaling of the pipes (cross-sectional area, relative to speaking length) not amenable to the necessary changes. I am reminded

Built for the First Baptist Church, Amsterdam, New York, by J. W. Steere & Son, Springfield, Massachusetts, 1893, this instrument was relocated through the Organ Clearing House and rebuilt by the Andover Organ Company, Methuen, Massachusetts, 1973, for the Pearson Memorial United Methodist Church, White Horse, New Jersey. It replaced a small electric-action unit organ.

This three-manual and pedal organ is now in its third home. It was originally built by Geo. Jardine & Son, New York City, 1853, for a church in Rome, New York. Relocated in 1974 by the Organ Clearing House, it was completely rebuilt by Steuart Goodwin & Company, Highland, California, and installed in Trinity Episcopal Church, Redlands, California.

of a fine instrument, built in the 1880s for a teaching studio and moved, on a very small budget, to a nearby church, where its soft voicing (intended for a much smaller room) resulted in a far less than fully successful installation.

Size itself—although some builders of new organs have "rules of thumb" about the proper number of "pipes per seat," as if that made any difference—is really not a major concern. I have played recitals on organs of scarcely more than ten stops in churches seating 700 to 1,000—in fact, one of my consultations on a design has been for just such an organ for just such a church—and I found the instrument totally successful. Numerous large nineteenth-century edifices were well served by very modest two-manual organs; in fact, I can recall two or three churches that are still well served by those same organs after a century or more.

Pipes, however, must be scaled and voiced to deliver sufficient power, and if, as in the case described above, the scales are too small and the chest space too narrow for the substitution of more generous-scaled pipework, the problem is serious.

It may well be, then, that only one organ out of a list of fifty available ones, meets the specifications and economic requirements of a church. It is not unlikely that the same organ also meets the needs of one or more parishes who have also been waiting patiently for such an instrument to become available.

If it is necessary to follow the procedure of the normal church bureaucracy, to convene one committee after another to pass on the purchase, or to make a concrete proposal to the church's main governing board, the organ in question may well be snapped up by another church in the meantime! It is wise for a church to secure advance approval from all necessary committees and to set the agreed-upon sum of money aside, so as to acquire an appropriate instrument as soon as it becomes available. The Organ Clearing House, by the way, advises and assists in the procedure.

Once the organ is in hand, the proper builder must be decided on to do the job. There are, in all regions of the country, shops that have a good deal of experience in doing such work. If your consultant feels unwilling to recommend one, the Organ Clearing House will do so. For this it receives no commission, whatsoever, incidentally. Often, an old organ is playable, but in need of mechanical repair. Whether it can be brought directly to the church or must go to the builder's shop for extensive restoration work is something that should have been determined prior to the actual decision to purchase. Usually, the latter is the wisest course, so that the builder may examine the instrument for any hidden problems that can be quickly and reasonably attended to while it is apart, rather than discovered after it has been re-erected. Usually, some tonal brightening is advisable, especially in organs built after 1880 or so. Those built before that are normally quite satisfactory tonally as they are, and no attempt should be made to "gild a lily."

Not infrequently the comparatively serious problem of cracks in the chest tables is found: a defect that often cannot be discovered if the organ is not playing, and may not be obvious upon initial inspection. Many fine builders feel strongly that such chests should be retabled; in fact, some builders prefer to retable old chests in marine plywood as a general practice. In some cases—and with some diffidence—I would disagree. Cracks can cause wind loss such as to make the organ unable to hold a tuning. If this is the case, of course, something must be done. Retabling, however, is very expensive. Sometimes a satisfactory solution can be found in inserting wooden wedges in the cracks: patching, as it were. Builders of less fastidious quality sometimes try to repair leaks by "flooding" the chest with sealer. This process rarely if ever works, and should be discouraged. If, on the other hand, the leaks do not affect the tone or tuning, it may be just as well to overlook them. Retabling, as stated above, is costly, and if it can be decently avoided, the money saved could well be spent in tonal work (unless, of course, the organ is already tonally fine) and in general renewing of small parts such as trackers, leathers and nuts, and even in the last thing often considered, cosmetic renovation: refinishing, regilding or stenciling of display pipes, new ivories for the keyboards, and stop labels for the knobs.

Much of the renovation and setting up does not really require the services of skilled labor. Any lay person can be taught to wash pipes, to vacuum interiors, to screw together case parts, to hand-rub oil into raw sanded wood, and to assist in other simple tasks. If the church can provide volunteer help to assist in dismantling and removing the organ (under expert guidance and supervision), if it can supply a truck to help with its moving, if it can provide laypersons willing to pass pipes and set up framing, considerable savings can be realized. A skilled craftsman, after all, receives his normal high wage, whether or not the work in which he is engaged at any given time requires the degree of skill he possesses.

Renovations can range from simply moving and setting up, as

was done with the St. Anne's Roosevelt described earlier, to a complete rebuilding of chassis, case, and pipework, resulting in an essentially "new" organ from old parts, still at a considerable saving. The extent of a given job depends on the organ chosen, the alterations desired or envisioned, and the amount of money available. It is necessary that the committee and its consultant have a clear idea of what it is they want when all is said and done, and that this vision clearly be their guide as they decide—perhaps on very short notice—whether or not to buy an organ that they have just been informed about. The Organ Clearing House does its best to match organs and parishes in regard to expectations, as well as budget and space factors.

It cannot be reiterated strongly enough or emphasized sufficiently that the work be entrusted only to a builder with a good reputation, and experience and sympathy in dealing with old organs, one who has a shop equipped for the task and an experienced crew of workers. Either the Organ Clearing House or an informed consultant/advisor can provide a list of recommendations. On no account should a semi-qualified local person—or worse, a well-meaning amateur—be allowed to tackle the job. Such a course has all too often led to disaster!

Four recycled organs. *Upper left:* Hook & Hastings organ, Boston, 1908; rebuilt and enlarged by Mann & Trupiano, New York City, 1977; now in St. John's Church, North Charleston, South Carolina. *Upper right:* Reuben Midmer & Son organ, Brooklyn, about 1885; now installed in the Prince of Peace Lutheran Church, West Claremont, New Hampshire. *Lower left:* Henry Erben organ, New York City, 1837; restored 1981 by Redman Organ Company, Fort Worth; still in its original home, the St. Paul's Episcopal Church, Woodville, Mississippi. *Lower right:* An organ by an unknown builder, 1840s; now in the Trinity Lutheran Church, Columbia, South Carolina. Note the reversed keydesk, allowing the organist to face the congregation. All four instruments are tracker-action instruments; all except the Erben organ were relocated through the assistance of the Organ Clearing House.

A one-manual and pedal pipe organ adequately meets the needs of The Church of Our Savior, Montpelier, Virginia. This tracker-action instrument was built by Mann & Trupiano, New York, 1982.

13

How Much Organ Do You Need?

The actual designing of a new organ will usually and properly occur after the builder has been selected, has examined the sanctuary and the area proposed for the instrument's location, and has agreed with the consultant and committee on a general scheme. Like any enthusiastic organ lover, the consultant may have toyed with a possible stoplist on paper. Indeed, very few of us in the consulting practice can resist looking at any sanctuary or auditorium we may chance to visit, whether or not it already has an organ, without envisioning what sort of scheme theoretically would constitute the "ideal" organ and then mentally working out the design. In fact, such an intellectual exercise by the consultant (or church organist) can make for an excellent starting point when the time comes for the builder and consultant to sit down and begin planning the actual instrument. The mechanics of working out a sketch of the stoplist will be discussed in a subsequent chapter. While some "sketching" with pencil and paper is useful at this juncture, no stoplist should be worked up with any idea of firmness or finality in mind. Still less should anyone develop a full design specification with such technical elements as pipe scalings, mouth widths and cut-ups, wind pressures, chest lay outs, etc. (even assuming that the consultant is able to execute such plans, and not many are).

Instead, the committee, assisted by the consultant, should ex-

87

amine carefully the musical needs, the worship practices, and the acoustical characteristics of the church and its sanctuary. When churches are seeking a new pastor, they often prepare a parish profile: a sort of inventory of assets and liabilities, of hopes and concerns; a coldly (it is to be hoped) dispassionate and honest assessment of where the church is, and a realistic plan of where it would like to be three, five, ten, or twenty years into the future. Such a profile is invaluable as a tool for collecting the church family's random ideas and ideals. It is also invaluable in allowing the parish to see itself as an outsider might, and to determine the kind of pastor that will best serve its needs (although not necessarily its whims!) in the years to come.

A similar sort of musical profile can be of value to an organ committee. When all is said and done, it is usually nowhere near as complicated a procedure for a church to change ministers (should it have erred in its choice of one, in spite of all the care it may have exercised in choosing a candidate) than it is for the same parish to change organs, once the necessarily large sum of money has been expended.

Numerous questions must be asked and considered carefully, and at the end of the process, the sum product of the answers may be found to point away from the type of instrument some or most of the committee members may originally have favored, be it a tracker on one hand, or an electronic on the other.

If, for instance, the kind of flexible and varied worship pattern that permits liturgical experimentation is favored, such as might well necessitate a sanctuary in which the furnishings may be quickly and easily moved, including those having to do with the placement of the choir, such must enter into organ consideration. A reed organ is movable; an electronic or electropneumatic pipe organ—given the acceptability of permanence for the speakers or pipework and a sufficiently long and flexible cable—only a bit less so; a tracker-action pipe organ most definitely is not easily movable, unless it is but a small single-manual instrument. Conversely, if the liturgical demands of the church, or the denominational form of worship, together with the structure of the sanctuary, are such that room for a pipe organ can be found, if at all, only by severe dislocation and rearrangement, such as to cause difficulties with the sensibilities of a large proportion of the congregation, that problem must be faced. If no amount of creative "brainstorming" can point to a way out, a compromise will have to be found as far as the type and design of the organ are concerned.

Of course, budgetary considerations will play an important role in preliminary planning.

We have thus far assumed, need it be said, that church musicians have been accorded the basic courtesy of a place on, or at least some input into, the committee that will choose the instrument he, she, or they will have to work with. Free and open communication among committee members, church musicians, and of course, the clergyman (who, in most churches is, after all, directly responsible for oversight of worship in the church) is of utmost importance. There must be frank discussions about the projections for growth in number and size of choirs, for instance. It would be unfortunate indeed were the organ to be located in a loft that lacked sufficient capacity to seat a large and active choir, or combination of choirs, that might be built up five or ten years into the future.

Because there is potential for personality clashes, a large measure of sensitivity is needed in any organ purchase committee. (I once heard the comment, within the hearing of the church organist, who was accorded a largely honorary seat in the group, "We might be able to get somebody decent for a change, once we have a good organ.") The consultant, being from outside the parish, and often the geographical area, can frequently be of great assistance to the organist, choir director, pastor, and committee in avoiding personal confrontations, focusing on issues and ideas that can be molded into a realistic vision or master plan for the near and distant future of the ministry of music in both the parish and the community.

The specific issues that should be addressed directly, are as follows:

Worship Is the church's worship format evangelical? evangelistic? liturgical? ritualistic? a combination of these, or somewhere in between? Is it fairly consistent in format and style, or does the church experiment with different forms, formats, and aesthetic ideas?

Use Will the organ be used primarily (or solely, as with an Eastern Orthodox parish, for instance) to provide background music? Will it give support to the choir? Will it be used to accompany congregational singing? Is there to be a recital series?

Given the uses anticipated, is a two-manual organ necessary? Many churches have gotten along quite adequately with single-manual organs, and a fine single-manual is both cheaper by far than, and preferable by far to, a mediocre or worse two-manual.

This small, one-manual organ in the Edgerton House, Hanover, New Hampshire, was designed to take up little space. It was built by the Noack Organ Company, Georgetown, Massachusetts.

Even if a recital series is contemplated, the great body of organ literature is eminently satisfactory when played on a single manual of proper design and construction. Moreover, there is a significant saving in space requirements (and costs) in a one-manual organ.

Choirs How many are there? How many will there be (assuming all goes as hoped with the growth of the music program)? Do they sing anthems? Is the repertoire fairly difficult and complex, with pieces that require relatively elaborate accompaniments? Are there children's choirs, or do the children and adults sing together in a "family" choir (a system with much to commend it, gaining solidly in numerous quarters over the separate "multiple-choir" system of long tradition)? Where does the choir sit: in a rear or side gallery? in the front, behind the pulpit or holy table? divided at either side of a chancel?

Programs Are plans afoot for a full-scale music ministry, with outreach beyond the church and into the community? Is there a parish day school, with a regular music education program either independent of, or revolving around, the church music ministry? Are there, or will there be, instrumental groups (many churches are forming them, at an adult as well as a children's level) and handbell ensembles, as well as voice choirs?

On reflection, it will become immediately obvious that the organ, if it is to be adequate, must be situated and designed with all the possibilities alluded to duly considered, although a well-designed organ of any size will serve the above-mentioned needs more than adequately. More germane, the builder must know and bear in mind all these factors as he works out his design. And it must be the committee's role, since he will not know the church that well, to develop and clarify, collect and pass on all the necessary information to the builder, through its consultant, if it has retained one.

Congregation Assuming, as is the universal case in most Roman Catholic and Protestant worship services today, that congregational hymns play an important part in worship, does the congregation sing with gusto, or does it mumble along at best, leaving the choir to inject whatever enthusiasm it can muster up into the hymns?

Is the congregation enthusiastic, reluctant, or apathetic about learning new hymns or new settings of the liturgy?

A new organ, properly designed, will go far to remedy congregational lethargy in hymn singing.

Sanctuary Is the sanctuary acoustically favorable to music? Is it lively and resonant? Parenthetically, if acoustical improvements are in order, the planning of a new organ provides an excellent occasion for doing such work. Some members of the church, and the committee, may quite understandably be reluctant about making visual changes; however, the very presence of an organ, especially one in a free-standing case, involves a change. A congregation can usually be persuaded to accept and even welcome other changes, especially when they are made aware that the proposed alterations will improve and enhance the effectiveness of the organ.

Is there a sound system in the church? Is it necessary for normal acoustical needs: music and the spoken word? Can its use be restricted to special effects, tape accompaniments, and the like? Will the acoustical improvements that may be planned in conjunction with the acquisition of the new organ render unnecessary electronic support for pulpit as well as choir loft?

Is there sufficient room for the proper placement of a pipe organ? Can room be made, if there is not? Must structural changes be made (even minor ones, like moving a door from one wall to another)? How extensive and expensive will the structural work be? Will the structural characteristics of the building that cannot be altered affect the organ if it is located as planned? Or, to put it another way, can the furnishings be rearranged to acceptably rectify such impediment but in a sufficiently *limited* degree so as to cause minimal if any dislocation or discomfiture to the congregation?

As these questions are answered, and the problems they address are delineated, it will become increasingly apparent to all concerned what the limitations are concerning the organ and its design: whether or not a tracker-action organ is practicable; whether or not the flexibility of placement offered by the electropneumatic-action organ is necessary; whether or not the even greater degree of space economy is required, such as to render appropriate the choice of an electronic organ; or whether the long-range aim should be a fine pipe organ, but the constraints of present economic conditions suggest the temporary expedient of a reed organ; or, given the small budget and the uses anticipated, a reed organ is the best permanent choice?

Not until the committee is clear as to the *type* of organ that is best suited for its situation can it approach makers or builders. Moreover, little is to be gained by attempting, as some churches have done, to set up a "debate" between a pipe organ representative—or knowledgeable organist—and the representative of an electronic organ manufacturer as to the merits of one over the other. In fact, most consultants and organ builders will simply walk away from such a situation.

14

Selecting the Builder

After going through the procedures described in the last chapter, the committee should have a fairly clear idea of the type of organ that will best serve the needs of the church. The ideal may well be a new organ, but the committee may find it more appropriate to the situation to contact the Organ Clearing House. If, however, funds permit and space demands the building of a new instrument from the ground up, the committee will now proceed to the next step in the selection process.

There may still be doubt as to whether a pipe or an electronic organ is the best choice, all factors having been considered. If so, the arrangements that must be made at the stage presently under discussion—committee visits and "auditions" of as many examples of instruments as is possible—should include examples of the work of one or more of the builders of electronic organs for churches.

It is advisable to hear an instrument at leisure, in a situation that permits its full range of effects to be explored deliberately and carefully. This allows maximum freedom for asking questions and moving about to hear the sound from various parts of the room. However, as was noted earlier, it is absolutely imperative that the committee subject whatever group of "finalist" instruments it selects to the "acid" test: listening to it function in a church service.

Once needs and limitations are adequately defined and the first narrowing of possibilities is made tentatively on paper as the logical outgrowth of the profile described in the last chapter, proceed to the next step of making arrangements to hear the various organs in other than the service atmosphere. Hear both electronic and pipe organs if one or the other has not been eliminated by either the distinct preferences of the committee or the equally distinct limitations of the situation.

Ask the representatives of organ companies to suggest installations in the area for the committee to visit. Insist that the organ be "tried" by the church organist or a member of the committee, or engage a neutral organist (or your consultant) to do the playing. Do not be satisfied with a demonstration by the company's representative. Nor should the committee be satisfied by the demonstration recordings that most companies send out at the drop of a post card! Hear the instrument live, and played by somebody who has no vested interest in masking any shortcomings it might have. Try to choose recent installations, in a sanctuary acoustically similar to your own.

Because it is difficult to retain aural impressions for any length of time, try to schedule visits in quick succession. If you are wavering between a pipe organ and an electronic organ, schedule a visit to each in the same evening, hearing the same music on each instrument. Such an exercise may help to sharpen the aural perception of some committee members.

A word of advice here. There will be considerable sentiment in the committee to rule out of consideration the work of any builder who has not installed an organ within a close-enough distance for the committee to visit conveniently. In principle, such a course is a sound one. Nobody ought to be expected to buy a "pig-in-a-poke," no matter how attractive the poke looks. Frequently, however, the builder who has not installed an organ in a given area is eager to obtain a contract so that he will have a "show" instrument in the region for other prospective client committees to visit and listen to. In order to secure such a situation, he may well be willing to give the church a very tempting price, even if he ends up taking a considerable loss on the contract. Moreover, since it is *his* "show" instrument and could, if a failure, be the last he gets a chance to build for a given locale for a very long time, he will not cut corners. On the contrary, he may prove exasperatingly painstaking in order that the instrument shall be as perfect, and the church as delighted as possible (and laudatory to others who may inquire about his work).

Fortunate indeed is the church whose committee stumbles on a proposition such as this. Some may be sophisticated enough to research out the builders of high reputation who have nevertheless not managed, for some reason or another, to make significant inroads in a given locale. I know of a large and superbly-built three-manual organ by one of the country's foremost makers of tracker-action organs that was installed for less than one-half what its contract price should and would normally have been, simply because the builder had placed no other organs in that area or in adjacent states!

But—and this is a *big* "but"—be certain that the builder enjoys a first-class reputation for mechanical and artistic quality, and that the firm has done a significant amount of work, even if it has somehow not managed to penetrate your area. Here again a consultant can tell you quickly whether or not such is the case, and he or she can be of great assistance in "bargaining" with the firm.

In fact, the company could well approach the consultant and ask, through him or her, to be considered. A "commission" for the consultant, obviously, is *most inappropriate,* and will not even be offered by an ethical company. The consultant, if he or she is a recitalist, may well have first-hand knowledge of the work of the builder in question from programs given in other areas where his work is located.

Returning now to the procedure at the point of "sampling" organs in the area, it is suggested that the first visit might well be one in which the committee listens to the organ as a whole, and attempts to get a broad idea of what the builder's tonal character is like. Every builder puts a sort of "personal" tonal quality into his organs, one that seems to transcend the differing acoustical characteristics of the rooms in which the several examples are installed. The church's own organist, or the consultant, might play a few hymns, a piece or two appropriate for a prelude and postlude, and possibly search out a few of the special effects the instrument might be capable of. Chimes, by the way, need not be tried, since organ builders do not make them, but rather order them, or install old sets, or install new sets in old organs, from the same one or two makers of chimes. Thus, regardless of what ears or imagination might indicate, all chimes are really the same.

In a pipe organ, listen for harshness of any sort in the voicing. Be aware of piercing brilliance rather than gentle clarity. Even if the church is empty, shrieking upperwork is a sign of carelessness in finishing. Do not be misguided by terms like "baroque style" and "classic voicing." There is no such thing in classic voicing as high-pitched mixtures without adequate undergirding. Baroque organs in Germany and other countries are in resonant buildings with high ceilings causing the tone to shimmer. Their effect is clear, clean, bright and exciting; not shrill and overbearing!

Listen also for unevenness between notes in the same rank, another sign of careless finishing. Listen to the attack and release for each note in a rank. These, too, should be consistent.

Pay careful attention to the full ensemble, and the various ensembles or choruses (groups of complementary stops) on each of the manual divisions. The Great Diapason, Octave, Twelfth, Fifteenth, and mixture(s) should be well balanced and build up to a climactic, inspiring chorus. Swell choruses should be less aggressive (excluding the reed chorus), but nevertheless cohesive. As you listen to the Swell ensembles or the Great ensemble with the 8' secondary stop as a basis (rather than the Diapason) and without the mixture(s), try to consider the possibilities inherent in the ensembles for choir accompaniment. Only loud and soft combinations are simply not sufficient; there must be at least a couple of gradations of volume in between.

Listen to the quiet effects, such as the Swell strings and tremolo; however, remember that no matter how lovely this or that stop or combination of stops is, it cannot make up for a poor ensemble in the instrument, for without a carefully designed ensemble, accompanying of choir and congregation becomes difficult if not impossible.

Keep in mind that special effects ought to be the last thing considered in designing an organ. If you have a choice, visit organs about the size of the one your committee is contemplating recommending. If you do not have a variety of instruments by a specific builder to choose from and must visit an installation far larger than you will have, keep one fact in mind. It is far more difficult to design an effective *small* organ, with a limited number of stops, each of which must carry its share of the responsibility for the instrument's success, than it is to design a successful large one, with a generous number of attention-arresting colors and effects. Listen to the ensemble. If the organ is larger than the one you plan to buy, ask the demonstrator (your organist or consultant) to draw only the stops that would be found on an organ of the size your church will be acquiring: a small two-manual, for instance.

Take notes on what you hear and record any strong impressions or criticisms that come to mind.

Going through such a procedure with a dozen organs is arduous, to say the least; nevertheless, the job is an important one and should be done carefully.

When listening to an electronic organ, follow the same procedure. Listen to ensembles, both loud and medium. Beware of any "murmuring" sounds, distortion, shrillness, dull-sounding fall-off (especially in the high registers) lack of a sense of spacious presence (especially in the bass register), and any unpleasant ambient sounds or static. Do not rationalize or allow a salesperson or representative to rationalize for you. Shortcomings are shortcomings, and a rationalization allowed could mean that your church will have to live with one or more of them, and that you will be rationalizing your mistake in judgment for many years to come!

Listening to several organs should enable the committee to narrow the list drastically. Maybe at this point, the group will be ready to determine that the instrument to be chosen finally will be a specific type of organ. Having narrowed the list to this point, the committee is ready to proceed to the other "audition": the step to which the reader has already been alerted, the most crucial one of all, listening to the "finalists" function in a regular worship service. Take heart, by now the number of "candidates" will probably have been reduced to a half-dozen or less.

As the committee moves into this next phase of its considerations, every member should have a clear idea of what he or she will be listening for and what he or she may safely ignore. In the latter category one must make allowances for acoustically poor sanctuaries, which will only be made poorer with the added sound-dampening of the congregation. The quality of a building's resonance is, of course, not the builder's fault. On the other hand, it would be well to note how successful the organ builder's effort was—if indeed he seems to have made one—to overcome the handicap. Singing is sometimes poor for reasons other than the quality of the organ. Because of their traditions, some denominations sing more enthusiastically than others. Episcopalians, for instance, are not as noted for lusty congregational singing as are Lutherans. In short, make allowances for differences in form and personality of various worship aesthetics. Do not blame the organ for an aesthetic quality which may not particularly appeal to you; but do not forget, either, that it is after all, *your* church with its own aesthetics that the organ you choose must suit.

Listen for adequate congregational support. Is there a liveliness and buoyancy of tone that seems to compell the man or woman in the pew to sing? Listen again for any harshness, unevenness, unpleasantness, shrillness, or lack of depth that may not have been so obvious when then church was empty.

Note how well the organ supports the choir. And finally, and maybe most important of all, ask that certain intangible question on which so much depends: "Do I like this sound enough to want to live with it for the next three or four decades?"

15

Contracting with the Builder

This is a brief chapter. However, much of the information in it will be of value in understanding the organ builder and how he works, and how to maintain good relations with him after the contract is signed.

By the time the committee reconvenes after having heard its "finalist" instruments during church services, it should be ready to entertain proposals from two, or at the most three builders. (Since the pipe organ is the instrument that requires the most effort and educated action, let us, for the rest of this section, assume that the committee has chosen to install a pipe organ.)

Try to restrict your proposals to those from three builders—or from two, if possible. Remember, an organ builder works on a very thin margin of profit. For him to travel to your church at his expense, spend the day there, make up a preliminary design, and then meet with and present it to your committee, may cost him well over $1,000 in time and out-of-pocket expense. Some builders refuse to meet with a committee, except for a fee, which they will credit toward the cost of the organ if they receive the contract. Although such a practice may cause resentment in some quarters, it certainly is understandable. Some other builders, generally the most prestigious, highest-priced, and frankly, most in demand (often five years or more behind in deliveries) simply refuse to compete for a contract.

If a church wants one of their organs, the church must come to them and sign the contract, after which the builder will visit the church, secure that he will not lose the commission, and plan the instrument.

At this point a competent consultant can be of inestimable assistance. First-class builders have no objection to working with a consultant whom they respect, and who knows enough to stay out of the areas that are properly the builder's concern. On the other hand, no first-class builder will defer to a consultant about whose knowledge he has doubts in any matter that could conceivably impair the instrument's effectiveness. Builders may remind their clients that it is *not,* after all, the consultant's name that will go on the instrument when it is completed, for better or for worse. The consultant can save the builder time and trouble by communicating details to him over the phone in advance of his visit, and even by sketching out a general plan from which both committee and builder can work. If the builder knows and trusts the consultant, he will use the plan as a point of departure and thereby save a considerable amount of time and money.

Two items must be understood by the members of the organ committee. First, although electronic organs are marked up considerably (dealers' reluctance to admit this notwithstanding), pipe organs are not. They are designed to order and custom built by the maker for the specific client. Thus, there is no real profit margin to play with, and bargaining—as in automobile shopping and horse trading—is distinctly out of place. Second, it is quite probable that certain effects will have caught the ear of some committee members: this one likes strings; that one, the Vox Humana. Do not try to urge or coerce a builder into sacrificing basic and necessary ensemble stops for special effects that somebody or other on the committee has simply fallen in love with. He will *not* give in (if he is any good) and sacrifice the basic building blocks of good ensemble; moreover, he knows quite well that your church would quickly tire of the "pretty" effect, as soon as the novelty has worn off. If you have a consultant, he or she will probably have his or her first of many collisions with the organ committee at this point, since the consultant will want to spare the builder the risk of bad feelings and the inescapable tension of trying to reason with a layperson with a fixation!

Make sure the builder knows what sort of worship service your church has, and what you will need from the instrument. Let him and your consultant reach an understanding as to who will do what, then sign the contract, and back off.

The rest of this book will describe the process of building and installing the organ. Some sample specifications will be discussed. This is for the purposes of background. The specifications are *not* intended as *givens* to be imposed on your builder or consultant. Nor are they models, from which you may try to design your *own* instrument, so please do *not* try to.

Also, do not do any of the following:

1. Get a specification from one builder (or a consultant—or even this book!) and then send it off to a half-dozen other builders to check prices. First, builders (and consultants) know each other and communicate, and they know the trick well. At the slightest hint of an attempt of this sort to get them to bid against each other, they will rally around their wronged colleague and purposely *overbid* the contract to him; that is, if he still wants it! Builders have a high sense of ethics toward their clients, and toward each other.

2. Don't insist on weekly or monthly reports on progress. There will be a long wait between the time the contract is signed and the first signs of activity at the church. Work and planning are going on, you may rest assured. Builders are both trustworthy and jealously proud of their reputations.

3. Don't suddenly determine that drastic changes must be made. Your whim can cost the builder money he call ill afford. For instance relocation of an organ from the place in the sanctuary it was originally to go is no small item from the point of view of case design and instrument engineering.

4. Don't drop in on him at his shop, unannounced or uninvited, just to "check things out." No builder has the time to play host.

5. If he is dealing with your consultant, don't "short cut" the process.

On the other hand, there are certain things builders would like their clients to know and understand, and consultants can often explain them more easily than can the builder himself:

1. All builders have delays, and churches must understand that no delivery date promised two years in advance can be a "hard" one.

2. Don't balk at a periodic payment schedule. It is standard in the profession. A builder is a contractor, not a vendor. He must buy very expensive materials before he starts the actual work on your organ. He must fund his shop payroll and overhead. More impor-

tant, the organ he is building is specifically for your church. If you decide to cancel in six months or a year, he cannot simply sell it to the next customer that comes along. The payment schedule, in addition to preserving his cash flow, also commits you to following through by imposing on you the same risk the builder is taking: once the organ is started, neither of you can cancel without assuming some sort of loss. Incidentally, builders rarely post performance bonds; they are simply too expensive, given the profit margin. I have yet to see a reputable builder leave a contract uncompleted. Moreover, builders as a whole are close knit, and should one be unable, through illness or accident, for instance, to complete a contract, another builder will pick up the work and complete it without change (except for the nameplate) and with scarcely a step missed.

3. Always remember that the builder has a vested interest in the success of the instrument. His suggestions on stops and placement are based on a good deal of practical experience and knowledge about what will and won't work and he has as much at stake in giving you a good organ as you do; maybe more, in fact, since no matter how mediocre the instrument is, your congregation will get used to it, whereas visiting prospects who might buy an instrument of his making will not.

4. Read the contract carefully, but don't nit-pick. Remember that the industry polices its own far more rigidly and with far more and better knowledge than can you. And if you have a consultant, he or she is watching the situation anyway. Many large builders use a standard contract form. If you have chosen a quality builder, no omission of this or that detail from the contract will make for less of an organ in the end, for he will not allow a contract omission to stand in the way of excellence. If you have chosen a poor builder, no degree of strictness in the contract will make the instrument come out any better, for the builder himself will have neither the integrity nor the ability to see that it does.

16

Some Elements of Tonal Design

An organ differs from every other instrument (with the exception of the harpsichord) in that variations in dynamic level and tonal quality can be had only by mechanical means. Whereas a pianist can increase the volume or loudness of a given note by striking or pressing its key harder, and the violinist or wind player can alter the qualities of a tone, within certain boundaries, by the way that that particular note is bowed or blown, an organist must do one or more of the following: (1) add stops; (2) change stops or combinations of stops; (3) open the venetian-blind-like shutters in front of the pipes (if a division is so equipped). Only through these steps is an organist able to change the volume or quality (color) of the pipe tones.

Thus, the decision of which stops, and how many of them, to include is a vital one in designing any organ, and an especially crucial one in approaching the plans for a comparatively modest instrument. The question is not so much one of volume. Given a basic ensemble complement of about a half-dozen stops, properly scaled, winded, and voiced for the room in which the instrument is to stand, a very adequate dynamic level can be had. In fact, even on larger organs, no more than a dozen or so stops are really necessary to build the instrument up to the "top of its lungs."

The extra stops in a larger organ are there for the sake of variety.

What one sacrifices, provided a certain basic number of ranks of pipes are present, with a small organ is a varied selection of tonal colors and "effects."

Some builders, especially the larger, high-volume firms (comparatively, that is; no organ builder has assembly-line production), and even organists, insist adamantly on a certain relationship between the minimum necessary number of stops on an organ and the number of seats there are in the church or auditorium that is to house the instrument. I disagree strongly with this view. I have consulted and played recitals on some very adequate and artistically satisfying organs of from ten to fifteen stops in churches seating a thousand or more, even though the builders alluded to above would insist that nothing less than three manuals and thirty stops would be sufficient for such an edifice.

Two factors that must be understood come into play here, neither of which relates to the comparative size of the room. Bear in mind that a single rank of pipes *can* be voiced to a deafening level for *any* room. Witness, for example, the "State Trumpet" in the gallery of the Cathedral of St. John the Divine in New York City. That single rank of pipes is at the rear of the nave; yet when it "goes off" nobody sitting at the front, an eighth of a mile away, has to cup his or her ear in order to hear it! The first question to answer is: what is the instrument to be used for? That question has been asked before, and nowhere is it more salient than in this context. Second, what—on any organ, in any room—is the *least* number of stops necessary and sufficient to build a satisfactory chorus, or ensemble?

The matter of use should always be the first question for consideration. I was once called to act as consultant for an Eastern Orthodox church, recently completed, seating 700 worshipers. It is one of the very few churches of that denomination that had determined, consistent with the care and expense lavished on the edifice and its surroundings, to have a fine pipe organ suitable to its liturgical needs. Part of the church's consternation was due to the builder's representative they had called in. He had promptly consulted a table of some sort and informed them that no fewer than thirty stops would suffice for a church of their size.

The representative neglected to consider that the Orthodox liturgy does not call for congregational hymn-singing, or for choir anthems with elaborate accompaniments demanding a variety of tonal effects. Had the church been the average Protestant denomination with a sanctuary seating 700, with a multiple choir system and an elaborate anthem repertoire, it *might* (although it most certainly *might not*) have needed an instrument of the size the representative was insisting on.

The upshot was that the church got its fine pipe organ, a superb two-manual with ten stops, which has served its needs excellently for over a decade. It remains the pride and joy of the parish. Incidentally, having seen the organ finished and having played the dedication recital on it, I can say that the instrument is also eminently adequate for the needs of a large Protestant congregation. Indeed, since that time I have seen almost identical instruments installed and used successfully in "singing" churches such as Lutheran congregations.

The question of the *least* number of stops necessary is but a shade more complicated. The one-manual Roosevelt organ in the chapel of St. Anne's Episcopal Church, Lowell, where I am organist and choirmaster, has been mentioned before. The stoplist, for the record, is as follows:

MANUAL

Open Diapason 8′ (can be drawn separately for the lower octave)

Dulciana 8′

Octave Coupler (doubles all manual notes played at the octave)

PEDAL

Bourdon 16′ (one octave of pipes, permanently playable from both the pedal board and the bass octave of the manual.)

The instrument serves in an acoustically alive room, seating about 125. It has only three stops, one of them a partial-compass pedal stop. The two manual stops are of such disparate dynamic level— one very loud and the other very soft, and both in the same "swell box" enclosure—that there is simply no point in attempting to combine them. One uses the Diapason for loud effects, and the Dulciana for soft ones.

This kind of instrument would not be designed by any competent builder or consultant today. Nevertheless, the fact remains that this 1881 instrument inspite of its limitations, has served satisfactorily two churches over the first century of its existence, and is now in its third home as it enters its second century. It is, in effect, two one-stop organs, one loud and the other soft!

Of somewhat more versatility is a single-manual organ of four stops, built by Darren Wissinger, of West Newbury, Massachusetts, in 1978, for Christ-the-King Lutheran Church, Nashua, New Hampshire, a sanctuary seating about 250. The stoplist is as follows:

MANUAL

Stopped Flute 8' (wood)

Spire Flute 4' (metal)

Nazard 2⅔' (metal)

Principal 2' (metal)

PEDAL

No stops; permanent coupler to the manual, playing the lowest 30 notes.

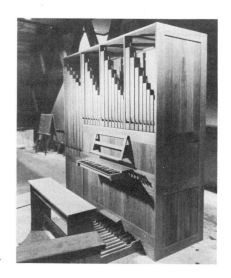

A single-manual pipe organ of four stops.

Here is a tracker-action pipe organ, in a white oak case with façade pipes made of solid cherry, that was less expensive than a comparatively modest electronic organ!

All its possible combinations must be built on the single 8' stop, the only one on the organ at normal pitch. Yet the stop is equal to the task. The 8' stop alone is voiced gently and suitable for quiet moments in the service. Adding the 4' stop to it gives an extra measure of brightness, fullness and volume such as to make a fine combination for accompanying the choir, and even the congregation at minimal volume. Adding to these either the 2' principal or the 2⅔' Nazard (which also colors the tone with a slightly pungent tinge), or both the 2⅔' and the 2' stops enables the instrument to support the lusty singing of a full congregation. Also available, as thinner but full effects, are the 8' plus the 2', and the 8' plus the 2⅔'.

This organ does, of course, lack the depth of a 16' pedal. Yet it is an eminently successful church and (as I can attest) recital instrument, and very much appreciated and used by its congregation.

Is the minimum necessary for the build-up of a chorus here—all from four stops? In truth, since either the 8' plus 4' plus 2', or the 8' plus 4' plus 2⅔' make for a satisfactory full sound, one *could* consider that there is, in effect, one *more* stop than is minimally needed on the smallest organ with any versatility at all; although, on a one-manual, four-stop organ, the idea of a stop to spare does seem to be stretching a point a shade!

What then is it, specifically, in the design of this organ, and others like it, that makes it adequate—even somewhat versatile— in spite of its size? The answer is, the systematic build-up of the ensemble. The fundamental principle is that it is the *chorus,* or ensemble, that must be attended to *first*; the special effects must be left until later. So each stop fits into the scheme of the ensemble and carries its own weight.

Were funds and space available, and a soft 8' string added, it would contribute little if anything to the ensemble—like the Dulciana on the St. Anne's Roosevelt, inaudible unless played alone— and would therefore be a questionable addition, given the economy of the instrument.

From these two small organs we may begin to draw an understanding of the importance of ensemble and the minimum number of stops necessary to create a good ensemble. We can also see the essential lack of relationship between the size of the room and the minimum necessary number of stops or pipes in an organ. What it boils down to is this: *Beyond the minimum ensemble, be it four or a dozen stops, additions are there for variety and not for volume.*

To overgeneralize for a moment for the sake of clarity, the difference between four stops in the Nashua organ and a hypothetical ten-, twenty-, or fifty-stop instrument, is the larger number of effects available, not in its sufficiency to serve in the building of a certain size and to meet the needs of the worship of a certain congregation. In designing an organ, therefore, one properly begins with the requisites for ensemble, and only after these are satisfied does one design in the variety to the extent that budget and other considerations will allow. Both the Wissinger and Roosevelt organs, it should be observed, are encased trackers and stand within the room, not in chambers outside it.

An instrument similar in concept to the Wissinger one, albeit a somewhat larger organ, capable in a modest manner of handling almost any worship or repertoire demand, is the 1978 two-manual Schlicker tracker organ in the University of Lowell's Durgin Performing Arts Center Recital Hall. The room is quite live and seats about two hundred. Its shape is odd: three stories high, but of limited width and depth. The organ stands completely within the room, at the rear of a shallow stage, and is encased, with front pipes of burnished tin. The stoplist is as follows:

MANUAL I	PEDAL
Rohrbordun 8' (metal)	Subbass 16' (wood)
Prinzipal 4' (metal)	Bordun 8' (wood)
Mixtur IV ranks (metal)	Choral Bass 4' (metal)

MANUAL II (with shutters)	COUPLERS
Gedeckt 8' (wood)	I to Pedal
Rohrflöte 4' (metal)	II to Pedal
Gemshorn 2' (metal)	II to I
Sesquialtera II ranks (metal)	

Here there are two manual divisions with buildup. On Manual I, the Mixture supplies the top and the filling out of the ensemble, as did the 2' and/or 2⅔' stops on the Wissinger organ. The 8' and 4' stops on the Wissinger organ and on Manual I are essentially the same in construction and design. Manual II has a smaller ensemble, however. The Sesquialtera, consisting of a rank of pipes at 2⅔' pitch and a rank at 1⅗' add a reed-like sound to the manual ensemble, and is also useful with the 8' stop as a solo sonority.

Obviously, this organ is not located in a church; yet, it well could be, and it would serve without change. Almost identical instruments have been built by the Andover Organ Company for St. George's Syrian Orthodox Cathedral, Worcester, Massachusetts; and by Fritz Noack for University Lutheran Church, Cambridge, Massachusetts.

Remember, there is no difference between a well-designed church organ and a well-designed recital instrument. The former is eminently useful in recitals, and the latter well capable of playing any sort of service.

The University of Lowell organ has the increased size and therefore the variety. A further increase in size would serve, again, only to provide more variety.

To sum up:

First and foremost, design for ensemble.

A one-manual, properly designed, properly encased and properly located, is eminently sufficient for most needs, especially if there is a pedalboard attached.

The number of stops has little if any real relation to the size of the sanctuary, as long as there is an adequate ensemble in what is there.

The organ, to be effective with the fewest number of stops necessary, must be properly encased and stand within the room.

My personal preference is for tracker action; however, an electropneumatic organ can certainly be built so as to be encased and to have the requisite ensemble.

The organs discussed in this chapter are intentionally chosen as examples of small but effective instruments, in order to illustrate the point of the above principles. The organs are very effective and especially suited to their ambience. An organ for your church may or may not have substantially the same stops listed; however, if it is to be effective, it must follow the principles as stated. The most successful organs of the past and present are built upon economy, ensemble, and placement. There is no way to escape it!

Appendix I of this book contains a number of stoplists of modest-size organs that are effective musical instruments—organs of all types. In each and every case, it will be seen that the builder or maker has provided the essentials of ensemble, and then and only then added "color" stops. In some cases, the ensemble consists of a full build up, 8′, 4′, 2⅔′, 2′, mixture and reed. In other cases, the reed is missing, or the mixture, or a mixture has been substituted for the 2⅔′ and 2′ stops. Such compromises do represent a loss; however, what is important is that there is adequate ensemble for supporting the congregation and for providing a full chorus of organ sound.

Electronic instruments, as will be seen in the stoplists, also begin with an ensemble buildup; in fact, one maker, Rodgers, includes in some of its models a pipe component—in effect, a pipe/electronic organ—in which the main chorus is constituted of pipe ranks and the softer effects, in which imperfections are more tolerable, are electronic. In principle, the idea is a good one. It is a heavy compromise, possibly one that many would not make. Yet, it is a carefully and artistically reasoned compromise.

Most reed organs, by contrast, do not often show a discernible ensemble buildup on paper, although the sound is there. My own instrument, for instance, an 1898-1899 Estey, is disposed thus:

MANUAL I

Bourdon 16'

Open Diapason 8'

Dolce 8'

MANUAL II

Dulciana 8'

Flute Harmonic 4'

COUPLERS

MAN. I-PED.

MAN. II-PED.

MAN. II-MAN. I

MAN. I Octave (doubles the notes played an octave higher.)

PEDAL

Open Diapason 16'

Stopped Diapason 16'

The reasons for the effectiveness in sound (lacking on paper) are several. First, reed organs were largely built at the turn of the century, when the taste was for a variety of 8' sounds, even in pipe organs, consistent with a repertoire largely made up of orchestral music arranged for the organ. Second, reeds by their very construction tend to develop overtones and thus there is essentially a natural chorus buildup. High-pitched reeds corresponding to high-pitched pipes in a pipe organ mutation or mixture stop, would develop uncontrollable and largely unpleasant overtones at still higher pitch. Finally, high-pitched reeds were not made in quantity and were not developed to the point that they could be counted on for stability and reliability, as were those of greater size, at 16', 8', and 4' pitch.

17

Building the Organ— A Sketch

The first step in the process of actually constructing an organ is the drawing up of a stoplist. This will normally be done as part of the contracting procedure, and the signature on the contract constitutes the church's approval of the stoplist and the builder's agreement to build the organ to that list for the price stipulated. There may be some changes as work goes on; however, in essence, the size and character of the organ has been set.

The list is drawn up by the builder, or by the consultant, preferably by the two in collaboration. It is *not* a specification, although one frequently hears that word used to describe a stoplist. A real specification includes pipe scalings (most often graphed, since few good builders today use unvarying scaled ranks), mouth widths, cut-ups, metal content, wind pressures, details of action, windchest construction, etc. These specifications will normally be prepared by the builder as his work plans. Although they *may* be and often are a part of the contract, they will probably mean little if anything to the committee members (or, for that matter, to the organist).

The visual design of the case is generally not submitted prior to signing a contract but is worked out as the instrument is planned in detail. Normally, the contract will stipulate that a drawing of the proposed design be submitted to the committee prior to its actual construction, for their approval.

In the matter of technical details, both those specifically described in the contract and those left purposely vague to allow the builder flexibility, it is important to bear in mind constantly that no good builder (and that is the only kind of builder any church should consider dealing with in the first place) will stint on quality for the sake of his own reputation, if for nothing else. Unless the consultant is unusually knowledgeable about the mechanics of organ construction, he or she should not in any way become involved in the day-by-day construction details. The consultant may be specifically invited to do so by the builder, or asked to assist in making a decision on some matter left to his discretion by the contract, or to act as a go-between to interpret some item from the builder to the committee, or vice-versa.

Contract in hand, the builder will use the initial payment that is made with it to purchase raw materials and such parts as are neither economical nor practical to manufacture from scratch in his own shop: items such as aluminum rod for trackers, set-screw held metal nuts for adjusting action, and squares.

He may also purchase the pipes, usually in unvoiced or at best, rough-voiced condition. Many excellent builders subcontract pipes to master pipe-makers, to whom they provide the necessary specifications, scales, and technical details. The builder will, of course, voice them for the particular organ on his machine and then finish them on the site in the church, after the organ is set up.

The wooden portions of the mechanism and wind system (either a main reservoir or two, or small reservoirs called *schwimmers*), the windchests, and the keydesk (although not always the keyboards themselves) he will make in his shop. He will also make the action. A builder who is overloaded for his shop capacity and therefore falls behind, may subcontract some parts—usually the action, or keyboards, or coupler mechanism, but rarely the chests—to another builder whose work he knows to be consistent with his own high quality.

The windchests will normally be made at the builder's own shop. Normally, they will be tabled with marine-quality plywood to eliminate the possibility of warping over a period of years. The trackers themselves (assuming the instrument is a tracker) may be made of thin strips of wood, or of 2mm-diameter aluminum rods. Some builders use fiberglass with success; however, I am hesitant about its

Most organ builders completely assemble an organ in their shops before installing it in its permanent home. This organ was first erected at the Schantz Organ Company, Orrville, Ohio, then installed in the First Hungarian Reformed Church, Munhall, Pennsylvania.

long-term reliability under the continuous stress to which trackers are subjected.

The pattern of holes is laid out on the chest toeboards and sliders for each register (if the chest is of the slider-type) are bored.

The blower is normally purchased from a supplier. The case is designed and the drawings submitted for the required approval. Once that approval is in hand, the work proceeds.

During the course of all this, the church is sending payments at regular intervals. These payments enable the builder to buy necessary parts, to pay his shop help and overhead, and generally to avoid a cash-flow problem.

Builders may have two or three contracts in different stages of completion at any one time. Large factories, those that usually build primarily electro-pneumatic organs and therefore can do more on an assembly-line basis, may have ten or twelve or more instruments in progress at a given time. (An attempt has been made to simplify, quite obviously, by focusing on the builder as if he had but one organ in the shop at a time.)

When all the subassemblies are completed (the wind-system, chests, pipes, action, case, and keydesk), the instrument will be assembled in the builder's shop for testing. Frequently at this time, he will hold an "open house," especially if the organ is being built for a church a great distance away, to allow his colleagues and local organists to see his work. The church committee and consultant, as well as members, will, of course, also be invited, and if they are nearby, should by all means attend. Acoustics in erecting rooms are by no means ideal, and therefore the committee should make no judgments as to the final sound of the organ from what they hear on the floor of the shop.

When the testing and open house is completed, the instrument will be taken down and shipped to the church for installation.

Meanwhile, the builder will have notified the church of the instrument's imminent arrival, and the church should be prepared to receive the parts and to set aside an area, as specified by the builder, for their storage. It should also have prepared the area that will receive the organ. If extra support is required (for example, in a rear gallery) structural reinforcement should have been done. If carpentry is required to ready a choirloft for the instrument, that should have been attended to. If necessary, a new 220V. A.C. line should have been run into the building to the appropriate position for the blower connection. Many states require that the actual connecting of the blower and switch be done by a licensed electrician. The church must make the appropriate arrangements for that.

Modern blowers, by the way, even for large organs, are quiet and small, and may easily be hidden inside the case itself. Long-since disappeared are the massive machines that required their own enclosures or rooms in some dark corner of the basement, lest they disturb the peace of the sanctuary by their mighty rumblings.

As may be gathered, the organ will arrive in fairly large pieces. Pipes will be in large wooden crates or trays; the action will be partially dismantled. The windchests, reservoir(s) (if *schwimmers* are not used) and the keydesk will be the heaviest single items. There is no avoiding the reality that pieces of organ will be lying across pew backs and on the floor of the narthex for a couple of weeks. Some items are prone to damage easily. Some people, for instance, cannot resist picking up a pipe and blowing into it, a practice that does not improve the condition of the pipes especially and increases the possibility of denting. It may be necessary to set aside a section of the church and rope it off as a temporary work and storage area.

The installation itself will proceed quite quickly. Assuming that the space and wiring are in readiness, the two or three men the builder sends will have the framing and chests up within a couple of days. The organ should take visibly recognizable shape within four or five days, and the first sounds, unpleasant though they might be (assuming the organ is not very large), should be heard within a week or so.

This is understandably a very exciting and fascinating time for the church members, the committee members, local organ fans, and numerous other folk, who will want to stop by and watch. Many builders have no objection, at least at this stage, provided that the visitors do not interfere with the progress of the work by asking questions, offering advice, engaging in conversation, or whatever. Not even the consultant's presence is necessary (nor may it be especially advantageous) at this juncture. The mechanics of putting the organ together are best accomplished by a crew from the shop that built it, erected it for the open house, and disassembled it.

About two weeks after the first crates are delivered, the organ should be together and ready for the final voicing, or tonal finishing. Usually the builder himself, as tonal director, will take direct charge of this operation. Often the consultant, if he is knowledgeable, and if relations between him and the builder have managed to maintain a degree of civility, assists here, for the judgment is an aural one, and it is the consultant who will make the final recommendation to the committee that the instrument be accepted.

In tonal finishing the pipes are subjected to often minute adjustments such as to make their volume fit the room, to regulate their evenness throughout the compass of a given rank, and to secure the desired ensemble blend. Then the organ is carefully tuned. Now all this can be a fairly long and nerve-wracking procedure, since a finisher may well find his ear losing its reliability, temporarily, after about twenty minutes of steady listening, and have to take a long break. Tempers are apt to get frayed during this process, and the best of friends can come to harsh words, or worse. Visiting organists, especially, and organ committee members, particularly those who feel that they can be a source of helpful advice and suggestions are quite apt to be dealt with none too gently, and had best be discouraged from "poking their heads in to see what is going on." Builder and consultant, though they may have worked together amicably for months, may find themselves in heated disagreement.

Yet at some point, somehow, (usually nobody present can recall the exact moment) the organ is done. Everybody present agrees that it sounds perfect—or at least as good as it is *going* to sound. In the next few weeks keys may stick, notes may sound out of turn, and minor mishaps may occur as the organ "settles in"; however, the builder's warrantee and reputation are on the line, and he will correct all these minor mishaps quickly.

Then, suddenly, it is over. The laboring and patient waiting of the last months is over. The organ is finished and awaits only the dedication service and recital. If the project has gone as it should— and that, after all, is what this book is all about—the committee will deserve the thanks of the church. The consultant will inform the committee that the organ is finished. The committee will inform the treasurer who will send the final checks to both the builder and the consultant. The builder's warrantee will protect the organ for the next five or ten years. But he knows that the warrantee is unnecessary; that he has done his job well and that the organ is beginning a lifetime of service that will far exceed his remaining span of years, as well as those of the consultant, the members of the committee, the parishioners, and everyone else now on this earth— and organ builders as a whole tend to live to ripe old ages!

18

Further Reading

The items discussed here constitute by no means a complete bibliography on the history and construction of the organ. They are, rather, a selection of comparatively accessible, very readable, enjoyable, and informative books and booklets by which a layperson can become familiar with some of the history, techniques, and "lore" of the organ. They will help a person do a more effective job on the committee, and may also awaken a desire to learn more because the whole subject of organs is a fascinatingly interesting one and well worth learning about.

"A One-Manual Sampler." Available from the Organ Clearing House, P.O. Box 104, Harrisville, NH 03450.

This is a thin booklet, containing a selection of photographs and descriptions of one-manual organs, new and old, and articles on literature for them, etc., reprinted from issues of *The Diapason*.

Barnes, William H. *The Contemporary American Organ,* 9th Ed. Glen Rock: J. Fischer & Bro., 1971.

Barnes's work has been the standard "textbook," if such there can be one, for introducing the uninitiated into the mysteries of organ mechanics. It is profusely illustrated with plates and diagrams, and written in a straightforward, no-jargon style. Barnes knew his subject, without a doubt; however, he is strongly opinionated in this book (and who *isn't* strongly opinionated about something they are familiar with), and several of his prejudices come through loud and clear, with no apologies. The information may be relied on; the opinions should be weighed carefully before swallowing lest they lie heavily upon the stomach!

Barnes, William H. and Edward B. Gammons. *Two Centuries of American Organ Building*. Glen Rock: J. Fischer & Bro., 1971.

A quick and readable historical outline of the subject, this book, like the last one, suffers from some strongly worded pronouncements that reflect the authors' opinions, but not necessarily the opinions of organists in general. It has some fine plates and sample specifications, and sections on all the main builders active ten years ago, almost all of whom are just as active today.

Blanton, Joseph E. *The Organ in Church Design*. Albany, TX: Venture Press, 1957.

This is a large, profusely illustrated, beautiful volume: a book one can page through for the sheer aesthetic delight of handling its high quality paper and binding and gazing at its more than five hundred high-quality black-and-white plates. Unfortunately, it is rather expensive, when it can be gotten at all. Most medium to large libraries own a copy, however. The book's intended thrust is to architecture, and the second section, "The Organ and Church Architecture," is very informative.

Fesperman, John. *Two Essays in Organ Design*. Raleigh: Sunbury, 1975.

A small book, but an interesting one. Fesperman's first essay relates the organ's design to its literature, albeit within fairly limited boundaries, as defined by the baroque period. The second essay traces the history of the "organ revival"—the return to classic principles in organ design—in America. Fesperman is an articulate and brilliant spokesman for organ design under the strictest of canons. One need not agree with him (I do, by the way, most of the time), in order to be fascinated by the concise manner in which he puts forth a large amount of material on the history and theory of organ design.

Gehring, Philip and Donald Ingram. *The Church Organ: A Guide to Its Selection.* Published by The Lutheran Society for Worship, Music and the Arts, 1973.

Church committees needed, and need, a small pamphlet with good, down to earth advice (the sort of thing this book has provided, it is hoped!), and this booklet fills that need in many ways. The approach is clear and matter-of-fact.

Ingram, Donald et al. *Acoustics in Worship Spaces.* New York: The American Guild of Organists, n.d.

The problem of church acoustics and architecture have been discussed in this book. The American Guild of Organists pamphlet amplifies some of the points, and takes some different approaches. Organ and music committee members—to say nothing of church building committee members—should be familiar with this publication.

Klotz, Hans. *The Organ Handbook,* 7th ed. Tr. by Gerhardt Krapf. St. Louis: Concordia, 1965.

Klotz's book is a step more complicated than this one in explaining organ design and construction. There are plenty of diagrams and photographs. The root philosophy, however, leans a bit to the strict Germanic, and committees of churches whose worship needs are not of the tradition will have to take some of the ideas with a bit of flexibility.

Ochse, Orpha. *The History of the Organ in the United States.* Bloomington: Indiana U. Press, 1975.

This is the standard historical survey of organs and organ playing in the United States from colonial times to the present. It is clearly and interestingly written and filled with pictures of instruments. Essentially, though, it is a history, to be read for background—and enjoyment and education—rather than a handbook of organ design.

Ogasapian, John and Carlton Russell. *Buying an Organ: Guidelines for Churches.* New York: The American Guild of Organists, 1976.

A pamphlet originally written for the use of the Episcopal Diocese of Massachusetts; later chosen by the American Guild of Organists (much to our delight) as its own publication on the subject. The booklet is quite matter-of-fact, and contains, in condensation, many of the principles discussed in this book.

For those readers of a technical bent who might like to sample organ design and its fascinating array of problems in somewhat more depth, two other books are worthy of attention.

Anderson, Poul-Gerhard. *Organ Building and Design.* Tr. Joanne Curnutt. London: Oxford U. Press, 1969.

Originally written in 1956, this is a heavy book, both in size and in content, and comes from a distinctly German classic bias.

Jamison, James Blaine. *Organ Design and Appraisal.* Milville, NY: H. W. Gray, 1959.

Jamison was a well-known West-Coast organ designer and consultant during the World War II era. His bias is distinctly eclectic, "American Classic" on one hand and English on the other. The book is somewhat easier to get into (and a good bit smaller) than the Anderson title, but very solid.

A Selection of Stoplists

1. The Church of Our Saviour, Montpelier, Virginia. Mann & Trupiano, 1982 (tracker action).

MANUAL

Stop'd Diapason 8'
Dulciano 8'
Principal 4'
Fifteenth 2'
Mixture II to IV ranks
Bells (a "cymbelstern," or set of bells mounted on a rotating mechanism)
Tremolo

PEDAL

Pedal 16', with the manual permanently coupled.

2. Lutheran Center, Pittsburgh, Pennsylvania. M. P. Möller, 1982 (tracker action).

MANUAL I

Rohrflöte 8'
Principal 4'
Mixture III ranks

MANUAL II

Gedackt 8'
Flötc 4'
Gemshorn 2'
Quinte 1⅓'

PEDAL

Bourdon 16'

COUPLERS

MAN. I to PED.
MAN. II to PED.
MAN. II to MAN. I

3. St. Patrick's Episcopal Church, Washington, D.C. Holtkamp, 1982 (tracker key action; electric stop action).

GREAT (Manual I)

Principal 8'
Pommer 8'
Octave 4'
Spitzflöte 4'
Doublette 2'
Mixture III ranks
Trumpet 8'

SWELL (Manual II)

Copula 8'
Rohrflöte 4'
Principal 2'
Cornet II ranks
Zimbel II ranks

PEDAL

Subbass 16'
Octave 8'
Octave Subbass 8'
Super Octave 4'
Fagott 16'

COUPLERS

GREAT to PEDAL
SWELL to PEDAL
SWELL to GREAT

4. St. Anthony's Roman Catholic Church, Upland, California. Rosales, 1981 (tracker action).

GREAT (Manual I)

Prestant 8'
Chimney Flute 8'
Octave 4'
Doublet 2'
Mixture IV ranks
Trumpet 8'

BRUSTWERK (Manual II)

Gedeckt 8'
Dolce 8'
Spindle Flute 4'
Principal 2'
Nasard/Tierce II ranks

PEDAL

Subbass 16'
Prestant 8'
Choralbass 4'
Trumpet 8'
Cymbelstern (See No. 1)

COUPLERS

BRUSTWERK to GREAT
BRUSTWERK to PEDAL
GREAT to PEDAL
Tremulant for all stops

5. Wyman Memorial Episcopal Church of St. Andrew, Marblehead, Massachusetts. Kinzey-Angerstein, 1974 (tracker action). This instrument was rebuilt from an instrument originally built by an unknown maker in New York City in 1843, and rebuilt by George Jardine & Sons, a major New York builder of the nineteenth century, in 1893, as its Opus 1088. It was relocated through the Organ Clearing House.

GREAT (Manual I)

Principal 8'
Bourdon 8'
Octave 4'
Fifteenth 2'
Mixture III

COUPLERS

SWELL to GREAT
GREAT to PEDAL
SWELL to PEDAL

SWELL (Manual II)

Spitzflöte 8'
Rohrflöte 4'
Nazard 2⅔'
Principal 2'
Tierce 1⅗'
Tremolo

PEDAL

Subbass 16'

6. Amherst Congregational Church, Amherst, New Hampshire. Andover Organ Co., 1981 (tracker action). This organ is also a rebuilding of an 1871 instrument by William A. Johnson of Westfield, Massachusetts, his Opus 342. The Amherst church is its third home.

GREAT (Manual I)

Gedackt 16'
Open Diapason 8'
Melodia 8'
Dulciana 8'
Octave 4'
Flute 4'
Twelfth 2⅔'
Fifteenth 2'
Mixture III ranks
Trumpet 8'

PEDAL

Open Diapason 16'
Bourdon 16'

SWELL (Manual II)

Gedackt 8'
Salicional 8'
Principal 4'
Harmonic Flute 4'
Flautino 2'
Larigot 1⅓'
Sesquialtera II ranks
Oboe 8'

COUPLERS

SWELL to GREAT
GREAT to PEDAL
SWELL to PEDAL

7. Trinity United Presbyterian Church, Indianola, Iowa. Lynn A. Dobson, 1982 (tracker action).

GREAT (Manual I)

Prestant 8'
Rohrflöte 8'
Octave 4'
Spitzflöte 4'
Nazard 2⅔'
Waldflöte 2'
Terz 1⅗'
Mixture IV ranks
Dulzian 16'
Trompete 8'
Tremulant

COUPLERS

BRUSTWERK to GREAT
GREAT to PEDAL
BRUSTWERK to PEDAL

BRUSTWERK (Manual II)

Gedackt 8'
Principal 4'
Koppelflöte 4'
Octave 2'
Gemsquinte 1⅓'
Mixture III ranks
Schalmei 8'
Tremulant

PEDAL

Subbass 16'
Prestant 8'
Choralbass 4'
Mixture IV ranks
Fagott 16'

9. Associated Organ Builders Model 340 "Classic" Electronic.

MANUAL I

Gemshorn 16'
Gedeckt 8'
Gemshorn 8'
Gedeckt 4'
Spitzoctave 4'
Twelfth 2⅔'
Fifteenth 2'
Fagot 8'

MANUAL II

Rohrflute 8'
Gemshorn 8'
Flute 4'
Blockflöte 2'
Larigot 1⅓'
Contra Fagot 16'
Fagot 8'

PEDAL

Bourdon 16'
Gemshorn 16'
Gedeckt 8'
Gemshorn 8'
Gedeckt 4'
Contra Fagot 16'
Fagot 8'
Fagot 4'

COUPLERS

MANUAL II to MANUAL I
MANUAL II to PEDAL
MANUAL I to PEDAL

8. Baldwin Model 625 Electronic

GREAT (Manual I)

Principal 8′
Waldflöte 8′
Dulciana 8′
Unda Maris 8′
Octave 4′
Copula 4′
Twelfth 2⅔′
Super Octave 2′
Mixture IV ranks
Chimes
Harp

PEDAL

Sub Bass 16′
Lieblich Gedeckt 16′
Octave 8′
Gedeckt 8′
Choral Bass 4′
Blockflöte 2′

SWELL (Manual II)

Gedeckt 16′
Rohr Gedeckt 8′
Viole 8′
Viole Celeste 8′
Principal 4′
Chimney Flute 4′
Nazard 2⅔′
Nachthorn 2′
Tierce 1⅗′
Fife 1′
Trumpet 8′
Oboe 8′
Tremulant

COUPLERS

GREAT to GREAT 16′-8′-4′
SWELL to GREAT 16′-8′-4′
SWELL to SWELL 16′-8′-4′
GREAT to PEDAL 8′-4′
SWELL to PEDAL 8′-4′

10. Saville Sovereign Model 8219 Electronic.

GREAT (Manual I)

Principal 8′
Bourdon 8′
Gemshorn 8′
Octave 4′
Twelfth 2⅔′
Fifteenth 2′
Mixture IV ranks
Krummhorn 8′
Tremolo

SWELL (Manual II)

Rohrflöte 8′
Salicional 8′
Voix Celeste 8′
Flauto Dolce 8′
Spitzflöte 4′
Nazard 2⅔′
Blockflöte 2′
Larigot 1⅓′
Trompette 8′
Oboe 8′
Tremolo

PEDAL

Principal 16'

Bourdon 16'

Lieblich Gedeckt 16'

Octave 8'

Hohlflöte 8'

Choralbass 4'

Mixture II ranks

Fagott 16'

Regal 8'

COUPLERS

SWELL to SWELL 16'-8'-4'

GREAT to GREAT 16'-8'-4'

SWELL to GREAT 16'-8'-4'

GREAT to PEDAL 8'-4'

SWELL to PEDAL 8'-4'

12. Rodgers Classic 200/205. This instrument combines a primary chorus of traditional unenclosed pipework with softer electronic voices. The tuning problems that are inherent in such an arrangement, and indeed frustrated an earlier similar attempt by another maker, have been overcome by an adjustable tuning control that enables the organist to compensate quickly for differences in pitch between the electronic voices and the ranks of pipes. An asterisk(*) identifies the pipe chorus stops.

MANUAL I

Prestant 8'*

Gedacktflöte 8'*

Gemshorn 8'

Stillgedacht 8'

Octave 4'*

Gedacktflöte 4'*

Fifteenth 2'

Blockflöte 2'*

Quint 1⅓'

Mixture III to IV ranks

Dulzian 16'

Krummhorn 8'

MANUAL II

Gedacktflöte 8'*

Gemshorn 8'

Gemshorn Celeste 8'

Rohrgedackt 8'

Principal 4'*

Nachthorn 4'

Nasat 2⅔'

Octave 2'*

Waldflöte 2'

Terz 1⅗'

Sifflet 1'

Scharff II to III ranks

Fagot 16'

Trompette 8'

PEDAL

Subbass 16'

Lieblich Gedackt 16'

Principal 8'

Gedackt 8'

Choralbass 4'*

Gedacktflöte 4'*

Blockflöte 2'*

Mixture IV ranks

Posaune 16'

Clarion 4'

COUPLERS

MANUAL II to MANUAL I

MANUAL I to PEDAL

Tremulant

11. Allen Digital Computer System 705

GREAT (Manual I)

Quintaten 16'
Erzähler 16'
Prinzipal 8'
Dulciana 8'
Hohlflöte 8'
Flute Dolce 8'
Octav 4'
Spitzflöte 4'
Quinte 2⅔'
Doublette 2'
Waldflöte 2'
Mixtur IV ranks
Cor Anglais 8'
Tremulant

COUPLERS

SWELL to GREAT
GREAT to PEDAL
SWELL to PEDAL

SWELL (Manual II)

Flute Conique 16'
Salizional 8'
Gemshorn 8'
Gedeckt 8'
Spitzprinzipal 4'
Koppelflöte 4'
Nasat 2⅔'
Blockflöte 2'
Terz 1⅗'
Sifflöte 1'
Mixtur V ranks
Contra Fagotto 16'
Hautbois 8'
Trompette 8'
Clarion 4'
Tremulant

PEDAL

Contra Bass 32'
Diapason 16'
Violone 16'
Bourdon 16'
Lieblich Gedeckt 16'
Octave 8'
Gedecktflöte 8'
Choralbass 4'
Flute Ouverte 4'
Mixtur III ranks
Bombarde 16'
Trompete 8'
Schalmei 4'

ALTERABLES

Four blank stop controls are available for each manual division. They may be set by means of cards inserted in a cardreader in the console, to sound various stop colors. The particular stop set by this means is erased when the instrument is turned off.

A Glossary of Terms

Acoustics: a. the science of sound; b. the total effect of sound in an enclosed space.

Action: the parts of an organ which connect keys and pipes; may be one of several types: tracker (mechanical), pneumatic, electropneumatic, or direct electric. b. the parts of an organ which connect knobs or tablets at the key desk with the chest, bringing certain ranks of pipes (stops) into readiness for playing.

Ancillary division: a division of the organ which does not have its own manual keyboard but rather is played from an existing one; sometimes called a "floating" division.

Antiphonal organ: from the Greek word *antiphonos*, meaning counter sound; an organ which speaks in response to another organ; usually placed in an area other than the main organ.

Articulation: the distinct speech of individual organ pipes.

Beard: a narrow roller or bar just below the mouth of a large pipe, added to allow the pipe to speak more quickly or improve the quality of tone.

Bellows: the mechanical device made of leather, which alternately expands and contracts to supply wind for the organ.

Block: the solid circular piece of metal in a reed pipe into which are inserted the shallot and the pipe body or resonator.

Blower: the electrically operated fan in modern organs which compresses air into "wind" for the pipes.

Body: that part of an organ pipe above the foot of the pipe; gives resonance to the musical tone and influences timbre.

Boot: the cone-shaped enclosure of a reed pipe which contains the shallot and its reed.

Breaks in pitch: the falling back of pitch to a lower octave in mixtures; serve to keep high overtones audible.

Bridge: a thin horizontal bar placed across the mouth of a flue pipe which allows the pipe to speak more quickly.

Case: the wood enclosure around the pipes, open on one side, which serves to give cohesiveness and direction to the pipe tones.

Chest: the large "box" filled with compressed air on which organ pipes stand.

Chest table: the surface of the pipe chest into which holes have been bored for insertion of the pipes.

Chiff: the initial sound of a flue pipe; may include inharmonic tones.

Chorus: a combination of stops belonging to one family of tone, e.g., diapason tone; also, the ensemble of a division, i.e., with its chorus stops drawn. See *plenum*.

Color: the distinctive timbre or quality of tone of individual pipes.

Collar: the "sleeve" on the top of a flue pipe which is adjusted when the pipe is tuned.

Combination pistons: pushbuttons located just below the keys or above the pedalboard; used to bring several pre-arranged stops into readiness for use.

Compass: the range of pitch.

Compound stop: a stop which sounds at pitches other than that of the keys depressed.

Console: the keydesk or case that contains the playing mechanism of the organ; includes the manual keyboards, the pedalboard, stop tablets and/ or drawknobs, couplers, combination pistons, etc.

Coupler: the device which makes various divisions of the organ available on other manuals or the pedalboard (intermanual coupler); the device which causes other octaves to sound (intramanual coupler).

Crescendo pedal: a large foot pedal which, when depressed, gradually brings into use all the stops of a division of the organ.

Cut-up: the height of a flue mouth in relation to its width.

Diapason tone: the distinctive tone unique to the pipe organ; from two Greek words: *dia* (through) and *pason* (concord), indicating similarity of tone throughout the compass of pitch. Also called principal tone.

Digital tone generation: development of tone by a computer that separates harmonics and represents them electronically as digits.

Division: a group of ranks of pipes usually playable from its own manual; most common names for organ divisions are great, swell, choir, or positiv.

Direct electric action: elements between key and pipe which are controlled solely by electricity; no pneumatics are used.

Drawknobs: knobs on keydesk by which ranks of pipes (stops) are brought into readiness for playing.

Ears: the projections on each side of the mouth of a flue pipe; by eliminating cross winds, ears maintain constancy in pitch and volume.

Eight-foot pitch: the normal pitch corresponding to the pitch of the key depressed.

Electro-pneumatic action: elements between key and pipe which utilizes both electrical and pneumatic devices.

Enclosed pipes: pipes within a swell box.

Ensemble: a group of pipes of one family of tones, one division of the organ, or the entire organ.

En chamade: the placement of pipes (usually reed pipes) in a horizontal position, projecting the tone forward.

Expression: the emission of organ tone in varying degrees of softness or loudness through mechanical means.

Facade: the "face" or front of an organ; in organ architecture, the arrangement of pipes in the forefront, whether pipes are in the open or enclosed in a case.

Finishing: the final adjustment of organ pipes after an organ is installed.

Flue pipes: organ pipes which produce tone when air enters the pipe foot, strikes the upper lip, and exits at the mouth.

Foot (of a pipe): the cone-shaped part of a pipe which supports it and carries wind to the flue.

Foundation stop: a stop which speaks at the pitch of the key being depressed; also a stop which has a strong fundamental harmonic.

Four-foot pitch: pitch which is one octave higher than that of the key depressed.

Free reed: a thin brass tongue placed within a thick brass plate, so as to vibrate freely within a narrow opening.

Fundamental: the first note of the harmonic series; identified as the pitch of a musical tone.

Great organ: the main manual division of an organ; almost always includes a diapason chorus.

Half-stopped pipe: a pipe having a small hole or chimney in the stopped end of the pipe.

Harmonic: one of a series of pitches in a musical tone. The first harmonic is identified as the fundamental; the second, as the first overtone. Every musical tone consists of a number of harmonics, although all are not distinctly heard.

Harmonium: a reed organ utilizing forced air pressure rather than suction.

Initial tone: the harmonic or inharmonic sound produced when a pipe begins to speak; sometimes called chiff.

Inter-manual coupler: the device which allows divisions of the organ to sound from one keyboard.

Intra-manual coupler: the device which allows the sub-octave, octave, or super-octave note to sound along with the tone of the note being played.

Keyboard: the entire set of keys on a manual or pedalboard.

Key action: the operating parts between key and pipe.

Keydesk: the cabinet or console on which the keyboards and other mechanical devices are placed. See *console*.

Languid: the "block" of a metal pipe which sends the wind against the surface of the upper lip.

Lip: the upper edge of a flue pipe, first impediment to the wind.

Manual: a keyboard for the hands, which controls one division of the organ.

Mechnical action: movement between key and pipe valve controlled solely by levers and other mechnical devices.

Mitred pipe: a pipe bent at an angle to fit into limited space; difference in tone is very slight and hardly noticeable.

Mixture: a stop of more than one rank that sounds various pitches; serves to brighten foundation tone by supplying additional overtones.

Mouth (of a pipe): the opening of the pipe above the foot.

Mutation stop: a single rank of pipes which speak at pitches other than that of the keys depressed. For example, in the Nazard, depressing the key for middle C will cause the second G above middle C to sound. Added to one or more other ranks, a mutation adds color.

Nicks: small wedge-shaped cuts in the front of the languid of a pipe; usually smooths out initial speech of the pipe and lessens harmonic content.

Octave: the interval between eight diatonic tones.

One-foot pitch: pitch which is three octaves higher than the pitch of the key depressed.

Oscillator: an audio-frequency generator used in some electronic organs to produce tones.

Overtone: one of a series of tones present (other than the fundamental) in a musical tone; number, loudness, and pitch of overtones determine the timbre or quality of a musical tone; also called a partial or harmonic.

Pedalboard: the keyboard of an organ which is played with the feet, usually contains 32 keys (two and one-half octaves).

Percussion stop: a stop which produces sound by striking action, e.g., bells or tubes (chimes).

Piston: See *Combination piston*.

Plenum: a. the total ensemble of the chorus stops in a division; b. the total ensemble of all chorus stops in an organ. (Europeans often use the term to refer to the ensemble exclusive of reed stops.)

Portative organ: a small organ carried or moved easily.

Positiv: a division of an organ characterized by originally a stationary organ as opposed to a portative organ; somewhat similar to the choir organ.

Rank: a set of pipes producing the same timbre, but each with its own pitch, one for each key on the keyboard, usually 58 or 61 in number.

Reed pipe: an organ pipe in which the sound is produced by a vibrating tongue of brass placed in a shallot.

Registration: the selection of stops.

Resevoir: the enclosure in which wind is stored; acts as a regulator of wind pressure.

Resultant tone: the tone produced when two pitches with an interval of a fifth are combined to produce harmonics lower than either of the two pitches.

Scale (of a pipe): the relationship between the diameter of a pipe and its length.

Schwimmer: a bellows-like device used to steady the wind entering an organ chest.

Sforzando piston: a toe or finger piston which brings into readiness for playing all or most of the stops in an organ.

Shallot: the hollow, conically shaped brass tube mounted on the bottom of a reed pipe, against which is placed the reed (tongue).

Sixteen-foot pitch: pitch which is one octave lower than the normal pitch of the key being depressed.

Slider: the thin strip of wood which runs lengthwise through the chest between the top board and the table. Holes bored in the slider correspond to toe holes in the top board and the table. The slider is the essential component in mechanical stop action.

Slider chest: a pipe chest that utilizes sliders to bring individual stops into readiness for use. Controlled by purely mechanical means or electrical devices.

Specifications: the listing of the components of a pipe organ, including number of pipes, scales of pipes, compass of manuals and pedals, chest-work, mechanical devices, materials used, etc.

Spotted metal: pipe metal which is between 35 and 70 percent tin, the remainder usually lead.

Stop: a rank of pipes, or, in the case of a mutation or mixture stop, more than one rank.

Stopknob: a knob on the organ console (keydesk) which controls the speech of one stop.

Stoptablet: a tilting tablet on the organ console (keydesk) performing the same function as a stopknob.

Stopped pipe: a flue pipe with its end closed or capped; lowers the pitch of the pipe one octave.

Stop action: the means by which stops are put into readiness for playing; may be purely mechanical, pneumatic or electrical.

Swell box: an enclosure equipped with venetian-blind type shutters controlled from the keydesk; gives expression to the organ division so equipped, i.e., it controls the softness or loudness of the sound.

Swell pedal: a large foot pedal which, when depressed, opens swell shades in stages.

Swell shades: the venetian-like louvers fitted into one or more walls of the swell box.

Timbre: the quality of a sound that distinguishes it from other sounds of the same pitch and volume.

Toe board: the board of a chest on which pipes stand.

Toe piston: a device placed just above the pedalboard; may set registration, couple divisions of the organ, cancel stops, etc.

Tracker: the thin strip of wood or other material which helps to transmit action from key to pipe.

Tracker touch: a degree of resistance given to organ keys so as to simulate the mechanical key action of an organ with tracker action.

Transposer: electrical device on some electronic organs which shifts the music being played into another key.

Tremulant: device which gives a "wavy" effect to the tone, actually the rapid repetition of a single tone. In a pipe organ the effect is produced by fluctuation in the supply of air.

Tubular-pneumatic action: an older type of key action whereby pallets are opened by means of pneumatic impulses (compressed air) admitted to lead or brass tubes by the action of the keys and passing through the tubes to the pallets.

Tuning wire: the small device which protrudes from the boot of a reed pipe;

used to change the pitch of the pipe by moving the spring which holds the vibrating reed.

Two-foot pitch: pitch which is two octaves higher than that of the key depressed.

Thirty-two-foot pitch: pitch which is two octaves lower than that of the key depressed.

Unit organ: an organ in which many pitches are derived from a very few ranks of pipes.

Unit stop: a stop derived from another stop of a different pitch.

Upper partial: another term for an overtone or harmonic above the fundamental.

Voicing: making adjustments to the pipe after its manufacture; may include cutting the mouth, positioning ears, enlarging the foothole, etc.

Windchest: the box of compressed air upon which pipes stand.

Windtrunk: the passageway from the blower to the windchest.

Wind pressure: air compressed to form higher pressure than the surrounding atmosphere, measured in inches (the distance water is raised in a tube due to air pressure).

Notes